"Jennifer successfully attacks the question of creating a fun and functioning home inhabited by Aspies big and small. She applies both practical detail and artistic flair, the latter often being overlooked in autistic spectrum people because of our devotion to problem-solving and perfection. This is a wonderful book to look at and to read. Neat freaks like me will find affirmation and the other half, those who have a hard time organizing their environments, will find solutions."

—*Rudy Simone, author of* Aspergirls: Empowering Females with Asperger Syndrome

"I really like Jennifer's positive work, emphasizing what kids on the spectrum CAN do. Jennifer teaches real-world skills that will help individuals achieve their true potential."

—*Temple Grandin, author of* Thinking in Pictures

"I waited for Jennifer's newest book, *The Asperkid's Launch Pad*, with great anticipation and I was not disappointed. Just as with the first two Asperkid books, this book is appropriate not only for the Autism Spectrum but the Human Spectrum. There are touches of genius in all of us. Jennifer manages to find the sparks, nurture the strengths, and address the challenges until we are left with nothing but focused intent and renewed appreciation for our individual awesomeness."

—*Kathleen Tehrani, CEO of Autism Brainstorm LLC*

"Once again Jennifer gives us insight into how Asperger kids 'tick'. A structured, consistent environment makes the world a safer place and home is where this starts. Her practical, up-to-date tips not only make home a safe place but a learning experience for life. The great photos endorse the idea. A must, not only for parents with Asperkids, but parents of all kids."

—*Dr. Judith Gould, Clinical Psychologist and Director of the NAS Lorna Wing Centre for Autism*

"With equal parts nurture and wit, Jennifer Cook O'Toole provides the recipe for superhero success at home in *The Asperkid's Launch Pad*. The accompanying photos invite parents to make small changes and teach independence skills that will make your home a safe haven. O'Toole's intuitive sense of what works best for Asperkids makes this book a priceless resource!"

—*Kim Fields, Managing Editor, Autism Asperger's Digest*

"Home is where your Asperkids become superkids! And here is the step-by-step primer to help make it happen. Once again, Jennifer Cook O'Toole taps her Aspergian perspective and wit to gift parents of these precious kids with priceless insights for success in life."

—*Craig Evans, founder of Autism Hangout*

"This book is beautifully designed…and the processes are broken down into simple steps. Jennifer is a wonderful example of being a successful mom and supporting her kids on the spectrum."

—*Robyn Steward, autism trainer and author*

"Finally! A how-to guide that explores a crucial dimension in the Aspie hierarchy of needs. An asperfriendly environment is paramount to supporting Asperkids and their superpowers everywhere. This book is a must-read for any Asperkid family!"

—*Tania A. Marshall, M.Sc. (App. Psych.), psychologist, autism specialist, and founder and Director of Sunshine Coast Centre for Autism*

THE ASPERKID'S LAUNCH PAD

HOME DESIGN TO EMPOWER EVERYDAY SUPERHEROES

Jennifer Cook O'Toole

Jessica Kingsley *Publishers*
London and Philadelphia

Photographs by Justin Smith on pages 22 and 149 courtesy of NFocus Charlotte.
Place setting artwork on page 51 reproduced with kind permission from
the artist, Jason Polan (photograph by Kristen Giuliano).

First published in 2013
by Jessica Kingsley Publishers
116 Pentonville Road
London N1 9JB, UK
and
400 Market Street, Suite 400
Philadelphia, PA 19106, USA

www.jkp.com

Library of Congress Cataloging in Publication Data
A CIP catalog record for this book is available from the Library of Congress

British Library Cataloguing in Publication Data
A CIP catalogue record for this book is available from the British Library

ISBN 978 1 84905 931 2
eISBN 978 0 85700 727 8

Printed and bound in China

**FOR JOHN...
HOME IS, QUITE SIMPLY,
WHEREVER YOU MAY BE.**

"Home is where the heart is."

Pliny the Elder
First Century A.D.

"Home is the best place because it's where my family is, and I love my family.
And Spiderman.
Yeah. Mostly
Spiderman."

Gavin, Asperkid, Age 3

CONTENTS

ACKNOWLEDGMENTS

This gorgeous book is the product of the talents of some very special people. Thanks to photographer Kristen Giuliano, who is responsible for most of the beautiful shots you'll see. Thank you also to NFocus magazine for use of the photos shot by Justin Smith. Remaining photos are thanks to Ellen Bruce, Torrence Photography, and my amazing iPhone (which actually makes me look like a decent photographer).

Thanks to Omni Montessori School and to Mark and Aileen Boltz (and your mudroom!) for sharing some beautiful scenery.

Mom, thanks for turning your place into small, plastic toy heaven so I could see my kitchen countertop (and my Barbie Dream House).

Maura, Sean, and Gavin: don't you ever forget for one moment that you are the best chaos on Earth. Always remember where your beautiful stories began and how much love embraced you here.

And John, may I never come back to a house where I can't find you waiting for me. You, my love, will always be home to me.

INTRODUCTION
Building Home

ASPERKID INTERIOR DESIGN

What makes us who we are? Nature or nurture? It's a chicken-egg kind of debate, and maybe the best answer is neither. It's a little bit of both.

An Asperkid, like any kid, for that matter, is hard-wired long before his birthday debut. His intelligence, his intensity. Her anxiety, her drive. That's nature. That's the brain and body which biology and chemistry concocted. And while the "wiring" of those of us on the spectrum may not be typical, neither, points out Dr. Temple Grandin, is genius. So, we could say that "nature" is the little person who arrives in the delivery room. It's largely "nurture"—the hows and the wheres of growing up—which determines who that person becomes.

What others see as stubbornness, meltdowns and tantrums are, often, the prickly points when Asperkids' hard-wiring intersects a world that doesn't quite fit. And it's easy to see why they need a refuge from that wider place, why they long for a safe spot designed expressly with their Asperkid "nature" in mind.

"Home" is that refuge, that safe spot. It's where children most deeply develop a sense of self, of collaboration, of stability, of worth; home is the beginning and end of the day, it's where specific experiences can build up to broader generalizations, confidence, and concepts. Home is the foundation for who an Asperkid will become and the choices she will make—both today and years from now. Sure. Good Asperkid "interior design" is about creating pleasant places, yes. More importantly, it's a *particular way of looking at the space* in which your Asperkid lives and making it the best it can be for ALL of you who share that home.

The way in which an Asperkid understands "home" (both as a place and as an idea) is powerful yet often overlooked. As you learn to see "home" as an Asperkid does, you, too, will recognize how a physical layout can either foster or inhibit deep concentration, calm, and a sense of control. That's important. Because in a well-planned Asperkid home, self-consciousness wanes, self-confidence increases, and eventually even "mundane" tasks develop their own intrinsic value.

This really is a book about home design. But it's not a color palette guide or textiles instruction manual. It's the explication of creating a home environment that teaches your Asperkid to believe in himself, to hone his concentration, to take pride in his work, and to build independence from the ground up. Then, he can take those skills, experiences, and solid foundation out into the world with greater success and satisfaction.

Your primary job as "interior designer" is keeping goals clear and feedback immediate, and matching challenges to your Asperkid's skill sets. A little stretch is good. Too much too fast is disaster.

Following the Asperkid's Launch Pad, the **place** you create will enable a **process**, which will foster a more confident, flexible, happier **person** who is less fearful and more joyful everywhere she goes. Together, we'll explore ideas for inspiring your child's creativity and thirst for learning. How? By weeding the garden, sweeping the walk, and using hangers. All these are multi-step, super-complicated sequential tasks (NOT an Aspie strongpoint) that others take for granted as easy. But when they don't feel "easy," it's awfully "easy" to think yourself stupid, worthless, or unimportant…when, as we parents know, our Asperkids are anything but.

You see, this book *is* about interior design, yes…but much more about the framework of confident, happy Asperkids than about the perfect master bathroom. We, as the families and educators who care for Asperkids, want to do everything we can to make life easier—theirs and ours. We buy what we're told to. We say what we're supposed to (usually). We drive to the therapies we're supposed to manage. And we try—we really try—to be the perfect blend of Martha, June Cleaver, Oprah, Melinda Gates, and the funniest/wittiest blogger du jour. That, my friends, is a whole lot of trying. And I don't know about you, but sometimes, I get awfully tired of trying.

Let's be honest. When days (and nights) are spent raising your family, attempting to maintain a marriage and possibly a career, unmatched socks and smudged baseboards are probably not the highest of your priorities.

"Alright then," you might think. "If she 'gets' me and my crazy life, why on earth would she write a 'helpful' book that assigns me yet ANOTHER job? It's just one more 'how-to' book, setting already-harried families up to feel even more inadequate."

I wouldn't do that to you, I promise. As a working mother myself, who happens to BE an Aspie (with all the overloads that entails), is married to an Aspie, and is raising three Asperkids, I know from my experience and from my gut that you don't need one more job to do. Like you, I know how tiring it is to pick up one more Lego brick (for the 75th time) when you just want to go to sleep. I know about the dread of purging old toys when your Asperkid may suddenly meltdown over an otherwise forgotten piece of broken plastic.

But, as an Aspie myself, I have also come to know something others might not realize: empowering our Asperkids—enabling them to grow into the exceptional people they are meant to be—does not require us to do even more. What we actually have to do—in very prepared, very particular ways—is less.

EVERYDAY SUPERHEROES

The type of "interior design" your Asperkid needs you to learn is more powerful (and a lot less complicated) than you could ever imagine.

This book, after all, isn't *just* about designing the interior of a place; it's about affecting the interior of a person. That's just as Martha Stewart's books on organizing, for example, aren't *just* about organizing. Those gorgeous "how-to's" provide worthwhile tips, tricks, and room layouts, sure. But they're just a means to the end; Martha knows that what we all really want—what generates billions of dollars spent on professional organizers and magazine subscriptions, and even smartphone "keep it together" apps—is **our need for mastery of our environment, confidence where we operate, and calm surrounding us as we do our work.**

Asperkids are no different. This world spends a lot of time telling our kids what they can't do well. They need social skills training because they can't keep friends well. They need occupational therapy because they can't tolerate noises well or ride a bike like the other children or write clearly. When other kids get to go to football or dance practice, our kids have tutoring or psychologist appointments.

We, who know them best, are privy to the burdens they carry. Despite their "super-human" efforts to blend in, the very amazing qualities that make them "super"—their intelligence, hyper-focus, precocious conversation, fierce loyalty, love of justice, and an amazing ability to recall gigabytes of information—those very same "powers" which distinguish them (wonderfully) as Asperkids also set them apart as "other." And they know it.

With a whole world telling them what's "wrong," it's up to us to show our Asperkids what is wonderfully right.

HOME BASE

When the runner slides into home base in American baseball, he looks to the umpire to hear the magic words, "You're safe!"

"Home" isn't really about bricks and mortar, about having the most updated countertops or the shiniest hardwood floors. "Home"—as an idea—isn't even an address. "Home base" means safety. It's a safe haven where you can find privacy and trusted teammates, opportunities to fail without shame, and the chance to succeed simply by trying again. Home is where the processes—of learning to be patient with yourself, to concentrate, to persevere, to finish a task from beginning to end independently—get to take precedence over the production of a finished, perfect "something." Home is where, in privacy, Asperkids get to inspect and practice at their own pace. Where they can develop the confidence and independence to become fantastic, authentic people. And where they don't have to be brave.

What does brave have to do with anything? Well, did you ever notice how so many Asperkids have a deep love for superheroes, fantastical (good versus evil) wizards, demigods, or space travelers? For those of you who never were Asperkids—take it from me, one who was. Every single day, Asperkids must be like superheroes-in-disguise. They "look normal." Nevertheless, just to function, they have to show more courage than most adults ever will. They have to endure almost constant sensory overload, fear of social mishap or of "being wrong"—and yet, they have to keep going back. It's no wonder times gone by or the Justice League or Hogwarts or Camp Half Blood or a galaxy far, far away seem more comfortable than their own classroom.

BUT WHAT IF I CAN'T DO IT RIGHT?

Asperkids are, by their nature, terribly hard on themselves. That's one of the reasons they are so burdened by anxiety and perfectionism. So here's a worthwhile question to ask if your Asperkid is paralyzed by perfectionism: "What's the worst thing that could happen?" Then follow each reply with, "And, then what could you do?" It doesn't take long to realize that a spilled drink, a burned dinner, or a broken plate is not the end of the world or a commentary on one's personal worth. Teach your kids to say ALOUD whenever an "accident" occurs, "No big deal. I can take care of that."

Your Asperkid is *very* well aware that *you* know how to do most any new "thing" correctly. Unless you routinely (and purposely) allow your child to see you struggle or fail (which you absolutely SHOULD do), all your Asperkid sees in you is a constantly perfect, omnipotent, "god-like" creature to whom they will never measure up. Then again, compared to that skewed persona, you probably wouldn't measure up either.

Sit back (or sit on your hands!), don't hover; let your Asperkid try and even mess up without feeling that his learning curve is a public performance. Be accessible, but not overwhelming. Why? Our kids have to know it's OK to be fallible. To be human. Just like we are.

Day after day, our Asperkids must go out into a world that doesn't quite fit. They are not only vulnerable to incessant criticism, they are also challenged by attention deficits, sensory defensiveness, and spotty executive functioning skills (planning and organization). Every day, they must be superheroes. No capes. Just courage. And us. Because no catalog or thera-putty or special educational "must-have" will ever have as much impact upon our Asperkids as the homes we design. The homes in which their stories begin.

Make over the interior of your homes and, in doing so, you make over the interior of your Asperkid. And while it may seem that our focus is on the place, it really isn't. Our focus is on the **process** fostered by that carefully prepared **place**, and on the **person** who "becomes" his or her best self within the walls.

SWEEPING? MY KID KNOWS THE ENTIRE PERIODIC TABLE

Asperkids are, by definition, uncannily brilliant. So it's easy to wonder (I know I did), are these "daily living skills" really important if she can recite Shakespearean sonnets at age eight? Short answer: Yes.

Here's why. Visually, emotionally, cognitively, Asperkids need "white space." They need order and structure. Yet because of their natural tendencies to get caught up in their own passions, the likelihood is that they more often unintentionally create chaos. What's more, theory of mind challenges mean that it's very difficult for Asperkids to understand the effort required by others to keep a living

space running smoothly. And if they are to move off to college or have a roommate, there are social consequences, too, of not cleaning up after yourself.

No home-keeping skill is too basic, and it's never too late (or really, too early, either) to start. The key is that everything must be modeled, taught, and supported with **consistent routines, clear expectations**, and **appropriate tools**. Experts agree that a two-year-old can learn to clean up under the table after meal time—*if* he's taught patiently and given a small dustpan that he can access, empty, and hang. A five-year-old can retrieve, use, and return a carpet sweeper and fold laundry. And a seven-year-old can absolutely scrub outside furniture, wash the family pet or mop the kitchen floor.

The goal here isn't a perfectly cleaned-out refrigerator and dust-free mantle. It's a well-prepared, confident person. **Through mastery of practical skills, your Asperkid gains the satisfaction of completing a concrete task and an important conceptual foundation on which he will eventually organize more sophisticated ideas.**

In scrubbing out a vase or hanging up laundry, Asperkids develop **sustained concentration**. In cooking a meal, they see the importance of **order and sequence**, and master **gross and fine motor skills**. In setting the family table, they increase their level of **self-care**, develop **better social skills**, and learn **greater appreciation for the work, objects, and environment surrounding them**.

Only through sensorial exploration and environmental interaction can children develop comfort in their body, in their physical orientation in space, in observable natural patterns and order, and our environment's inclination to control error through predictable cause-and-effect experiences. You have to feel the sand between your toes before you can wonder at the pull of the moon on the tides, the artistic relationship between sea and shore, or the chain of life involving the inhabitants of shells sloshing around your feet. And once you wonder, you will be compelled to ask questions of other people. To interact. To communicate.

It all begins with the **real, concrete world** around our children. People—by our nature—don't joyfully (or successfully) absorb knowledge by force. Sure, we can use rote memory techniques to help us along, but if facts are merely unconnected trivia bits, they won't matter much, and they certainly won't be remembered. What we, as human beings, do best is to mess around with, poke, turn over, stroke, and generally "manipulate" the real

sights, sounds, scents, touches, and tastes that make up our world. From that concrete foundation, developing brains fashion a framework for more sophisticated intellectual and social skills AND retain them because we have seen how they make sense in the REAL world.

Asperkids have to discover these experiences for themselves. We cannot do it for them, nor can we lecture it into their fingertips, vision, or joints. We can, however, give them the tools, repetition, and exposure they need to succeed. And as our children (of all ages) are able to ground themselves in the most basic, elemental, sensorial experiences of all—those which exist in the natural world—they can and will move on to more. To wonder and hypothesis. To concentration and responsibility. To contribute their own mental superpowers to the greater world.

But first we must help our Asperkids experience **"being" through "doing"** in a home that suits their needs: a lack of clutter and space to move without obstacles or having their concentration disturbed. Simplicity, order, beauty, calm have to reign. Asperkids need the clarity and reliability of a lovingly structured environment where obstacles have been removed and resources thoughtfully provided.

Then, you get to see the best reward ever… the bright smile of a young person (be he 3 or 13) that says, **"Actually, I can."**

THE PLACE AND THE PROCESS

In every room, in every space, there are **three basic steps**—concepts—for you to apply. The result will ALWAYS be a safer, more pleasant, aesthetically pleasing, creativity-, confidence-, and calm-inducing "launch pad" in which your Asperkid will discover—at his own pace—his own best self.

In the illustrations in this section, notice the real (smaller-sized) hammers, wrench, vise, screwdrivers, safety goggles, work aprons, sanding blocks, and so on, all of which are alongside Dad's actual tool bench and made accessible to the youngest kiddo by the simple inclusion of a step stool.

Step 1—Prepare an environment that considers the physical and emotional needs of your Asperkid (uncluttered areas where easy movement is possible, and "real" tools are accessible, and authentic—rather than "pretend"—materials are used).

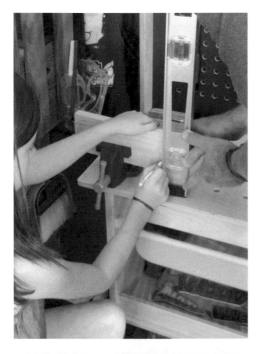

Step 2—In slow, step-by-step lessons, take the time to gradually teach your Asperkid how to use the tools and space you've supplied (many "basic" skills are more layered and complex than they seem).

Step 3—Then, allow your Asperkid the freedom to try those new skills independently (and to fail, and try again) tempered by your availability, if needed, and the structure needed to learn (safely and confidently).

And that's it. The design formula for the place and the person, for the foundation, the launch pad, the HOME our Asperkids need. You don't need to know a thing about color matching or feng shui. All you have to know is that the interior you design is far, far more important than anything off the pages of *House Beautiful*. After all, you're designing the interior of a person.

From the layout of the kitchen pantry to the extended bedroom light switch—small adjustments add up to one grandly important "process." That's why "home design" for an Asperkid has nothing to do with fabric swatches, and everything to do with a thoughtful adult creating the space which will make possible the process of "becoming." It's lovely. It's doable. And it doesn't require a whole bunch of gadgets or gizmos.

Our Asperkids can be super-brave, super-resilient, super-grounded "superheroes" every single day, because success is simpler to come by than marketing folks would have us believe... So, welcome "home."

C'mon. Let's take a look around...

PART 1

THE PLACE

WHERE ASPERKIDS BECOME SUPERHEROES...EVERY DAY

PUBLIC SPACES

Playrooms and Family Rooms, the Kitchen, the Launch Pad, and Tidying Up

Some Asperkids live in high-rise apartments. Others on farms. Still others call suburbia "home." No one-size-fits-all prescription will fit the needs of every family structure or every physical structure. That's perfectly fine. After all, no Asperkid is one-size-fits-all anyway.

The particulars of your space will, of course, dictate square footage and how much or little you can change what already "is." Some homes include entire craft rooms; some apartment dwellers wouldn't want a craft room even if space allowed. So take what you love and leave the rest, because the "best" part of preparing the public spaces is that your efforts will actually pay off for every family member.

Take the time to guide your Asperkid through any new routines, layouts, and responsibilities. And other than that—just one more "preparation" instruction: prepare... to have fun.

A PLACE TO PLAY

No matter what the particular dimensions of your home or ages in your family, every Asperkid home requires a common space where the main purpose is shared leisure time. Aspies don't like small talk, collaboration is tough, and they aren't naturally inclined to ask family members about their own goings-on. That's where you, interior designer, come in.

In order to keep a job or make a friend, to get a date or win a client, we, Aspies, have to learn to "play" alongside others: taking turns choosing the background music or activity, politely sharing space with those around us. Call it in-home social skills training, but be it an entire room or a portion of the general family/living room—some part of your home must create a space for collaboration and interaction "just because."

PREPARE THE SPACE, PREPARE THE ASPERKID

- No one interacts as well when a screen is lit up. Not even neurotypical (NTs).

- Rotate. Change out the toys, books, puzzles or games on display. Store them out of sight for a while, and bring them back in a few months' time. During the absence, your Asperkid will develop new skills and insights and will find new ways of interacting with whatever you present.

- Include books of artwork or photography that are "above" your Asperkid. Learning is a bit like tennis. Children will "play up" to the tone of ideas and images which surround them, developing questions about and appreciation for subjects far "ahead" of their years.

- Leave some wiggle room. Really. Asperkids need vestibular input (movement) to regulate themselves; build it into your home design and everyone (parents included) will feel a whole lot calmer. Save your couch from "crashing" damage by adding a small trampoline, "active" games (from classics like Twister to Wii Fit Dance Party), rocking chairs, a hoppy ball, a punching bag or giant beanbag chairs.

- Stick up a magnetic bulletin board, or a thin towel bar with hooks and hanging cups. An under-the-shelf hanging wine rack can become a pens/pencils/markers/highlighters holder.

- Fill common spaces with items that will spark conversations and interest in adults and kids alike: maps, puzzles, games, sand art, plants and flowers, personal mementos to generate story-telling, containers to open/close, books of every kind, models, and activities that are interesting to explore alone or together.

Cubbies give a place for everything and make it easy to return everything to its place.

- Place smaller items or collections on trays, in open baskets, or in clear boxes to create cohesiveness.

- Encourage "together" time with board games and easily reached art supplies (try molecular or historic coloring books as incentives), stamping, magnetic blocks, and giant floor puzzles.

THE FAMILY THAT PLAYS TOGETHER: OLD-SCHOOL "FAMILY ROOM" FUN, NEW-SCHOOL "ASPERKID" LOGIC

The most important cabinet in your home may not be the one holding Grandma's silver, and the most important closet may not contain fur coats or family heirlooms. When it comes to helping our Asperkids develop the skills they need to function successfully in the world, the most important storage spot in your home is the family Game Closet.

I can hear you laughing. Or maybe that was an audible wince. "Seriously?" you may be rolling your eyes. "Seriously? She's telling me to make sure we have a *game closet?*" Yes, my friends, seriously. Very seriously. And here's why.

To Asperkids, there is only winner or loser, only right or wrong, all or nothing. That's called "rigid" or inflexible thinking, and it's at the heart of so many of the "behaviors" the world doesn't like in our kids. Rigid thinking interferes with:

- accepting advice (or, in their case, not accepting it)

- trying out new foods, activities, and experiences

- shifting activities: leaving playdates, getting out of the house to school

- handling frustrations when the going gets rough

- losing a game or facing disappointment

- moving smoothly from one school-day activity to another

- adjusting to changes in routines, places, and people.

Know this for sure: your Asperkid's inflexibility is *based in fear, not rebellion*, but the fact remains: if Aspies are going to get better at writing essays, develop sports techniques, partner with our spouses, or accept constructive criticism from an employer, we can't take a "my way or the highway" approach.

GAMING

While collaborative, cooperative, group play seems easy and fun to NTs—it's REALLY tough work for Asperkids. It's also really important.

Grab a blindfold or some dice and turn your home's common spaces into mind-stretching zones.

Want to know just a few of the skills you can practice right there on the coffee table? How about…

- turn-taking

- losing as part of a team, even when you've played well

- delayed gratification ("You might win next round.")

- working with a teammate on shared goals

- managing disappointment

- developing "working memory" (holding information at the ready while using or changing it)

- focus and attentiveness

- negotiating conflicts.

Collaborative, cooperative, group play is easy and fun to NTs—but you can see how it's REALLY tough work for our Asperkids. And that is why it's so important that you carve out the space (and the time) to practice.

THE HOW-TOS

- Grab an ordinary household item and play "What is it?" In no particular order, players pick up the item and imagine the ridiculous things "it" could be (e.g. a potato masher could be an alien antenna or a metal detector). The crazier the better.

- Play act what it looks like to be a sore loser, a "sore winner," and a gracious friend. Ham it up! Get some laughs! No one likes a lecture.

- Begin with games of pure chance (like Chutes and Ladders or Candy Land, Zingo, "war" with a deck of cards), then SLOWLY add strategic games like Rush Hour, Password, chess, Risk, Swish, Qwirkle, Headbands, Gobblet, Dizios.

- Classics like charades, Blindman's Bluff, Simon Says, and Twister challenge sensory work and are really, really FUN.

- Remind your Asperkids that "Everything is hard before it's easy," and that "What's easy for one person isn't always easy for another." If another player seems to be struggling, gently offer to help or just wait patiently without making judgments.

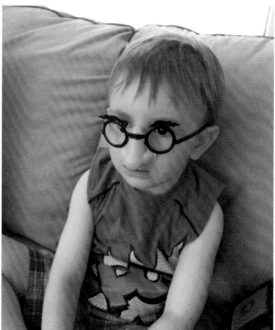

- Asperkids are still KIDS. But sometimes, they need a little reminder that it's OK to take life (and themselves) a little less seriously... So, above all, don't forget to practice having FUN!

Sort It Out: Make Shared Spaces MAKE SENSE!

Group activities **by subject**: an art corner here (supplies, photo books, pottery), and the science over there (microscope and slides with the Discovery Channel DVDs).

OR

Organize the space **by theme** (my favorite method because it encourages "accidental" exploration): place books on Van Gogh's paintings next to a flower press, a live plant, science books on plant cells with a microscope, a copy of *The Secret Garden*, and botanical puzzles.

ALL GOOD PARTIES END UP IN THE KITCHEN

"Home is where your story begins"—I don't know who first said that, but it's true. The place to learn self-confidence (or the lack thereof) is at home—and more than anywhere else, the heart of your home is your kitchen.

Star-charts pasted to the fridge, doodles taped to the wall—those are all affirming and great. But authentically involving Asperkids in real "home work"—through demonstration, expectation, and preparation—is the ultimate proof of your belief in their potential, their value to "the team," and the smile you get from their one-of-a-kind company.

No matter how big (or small) your home may be, the kitchen is the one place where everyone seems to congregate. It's where memories are made and conversations flow. And what matters much, much more than the choice of countertop or backsplash is how well the space supports the movement, communication, and independence of the folks who use it. ALL of them. And that most definitely includes your Asperkids.

38 STEPS TO ORANGE JUICE

Adults often assume that since Asperkids are so bright, they can do everything easily. That's just not true—and it's not fair. In fact, more often than not, we adults are the ones to blame, as we often fail to provide our kids the space, tools, instruction, and practice they need to become independent. Reluctant Asperkids are not being lazy when they ask for help instead of problem-solving for themselves; given the proper tools, accessibility, and instruction, there's nothing they can't do. But first: prepare the space, prepare the Asperkid, and then give it a go.

Step 1—Prepare the space. Even the smallest self-help skill—like getting a drink when you are thirsty—contains lots of little steps for a less-than-coordinated body.

Asperkids are already a bit intimidated by a new task; then, if like Alice in Wonderland, everything is five times too big or too tall or too heavy, you've got a sure recipe for disaster. Gross motor planning and fine motor control are big challenges for our kids. If your Asperkid is young or small, provide materials that "fit" his body.

Step 2—Prepare the Asperkid. Give demonstrations for ALL new jobs. Our children need to see every stage of an activity (as well as the end product) before ever being asked to attempt it themselves.

Step 3—Give it a go. Once the stage is set and the "players" are well rehearsed, it's time to let your Asperkid try independently.

What does that look like? Let me set up a scene for you: when my three-year-old Asperkid says, "Mommy, I'm thirsty," my reply is, "OK. What can you do about that?" (Don't supply the answer!) Usually, he giggles as the solution occurs to him. "Oh! I can get a drink!" And he does—independently, which is a REALLY big deal. Even after he's thought of getting that drink, just consider how many steps and skills that task involves:

1. He goes to the "kids' cabinet."

2. He opens the door.

3. He slides out the shelf (he's already learned what happens if he rolls those casters too quickly!).

4. He picks out to his own child-sized glass (yes, glass, not a plastic cup).

5. He slides the shelf back in, listening for glass clanking to tell if he's been too rough.

6. He closes the door.

7. He walks to the kitchen table.

8. He places the glass on his placemat.

9. He walks to the refrigerator.

10. He opens the door.

11. He grabs the juice pitcher (which is child-sized, glass, lidded, and on the bottom shelf) and sets it on the counter.

12. He closes the door and picks up the pitcher.

13. He carries the pitcher to the table.

14. He places the pitcher on his placemat.

15. He pulls out his chair.

16. He sits.

17. He pours the juice in the way that he's been taught—tipping only when the spout is over the center of the glass, supporting it with his "helper hand," and listening to be certain he doesn't "clink" the glass.

18. He stops pouring when he can see the glass is full enough.

19. He places the juice down.

20. He drinks.

21. When he's through, he pushes out his chair.

22. He stands up.

23. He pushes his chair back in.

24. With two hands, he picks up the pitcher.

25. He carries it to the fridge.

26. He places it on the countertop.

27. He opens the refrigerator.

28. He retrieves the pitcher.

29. He places it in its spot.

30. He closes the door.

31. He walks back for his glass.

32. He retrieves the glass, carrying it away from the table.

33. He places it on the countertop.

34. He opens the dishwasher.

35. He slides out the top drawer.

36. He places the glass face-down without hitting any other items.

37. He slides the drawer back in.

38. He closes the dishwasher. And…ta-da! Done!

LET'S GET COOKIN'

From kids' pantries to manageable seating, from the homemade vase to the dinner table your Asperkid sets, your kitchen layout must say, "You are part of this team. Your contributions matter and are necessary." After all, our homes belong to us. ALL of us. Asperkids (always) included.

PREPARE THE SPACE

- Accessibility: if they can't see it, reach it or carry it, they won't use it. Fill the lowest few pantry shelves with the snack choices you want your kiddos to eat.

- Take cereal bars, dried fruit pouches, nuts, wholegrain crackers, and so on out of difficult-to-open or reseal bags or boxes, and transfer them to see-through containers or stand them up in open coffee mugs.

- Store water bottles and lunch boxes here, too, so your Asperkid can prepare his school meal.

- Set aside a low shelf (or two) on the door of your refrigerator where you can stock the drinks you want consumed—choose light milk or juice cartons for greater control, or try pre-pouring juice into a small, lidded pitcher.

- Take perishable snacks out of larger bags or snack-packs (breaking apart individual yogurt or pudding cups, for example) and set them on another low shelf. Place cleaned, portioned produce (baby carrots, grape tomatoes) in see-through lidded containers.

- Store deli meats, olives, pre-washed fruit chunks or veggie sticks in lidded plasticware that you turn UPSIDE-DOWN (your Asperkid can better see the contents and grab these easy snacks).

- Take anything that's tall and long out of tough-to-open bags (like individually wrapped mozzarella cheese sticks), and pop the lot of them into a tall cup for anyone to grab without being encumbered by packaging struggles.

- Create a "kids' cabinet" that is independently reachable by ALL young people.

- Fill it with REAL glasses, silverware, and plates (their weight conveys their value and your trust).

- Keep silverware in clearly compartmentalized organizers or baskets.

- Make eating easier. Provide utensils, plates, and glasses that are scaled correctly for your Asperkid's hands.

- REAL, manageable kitchen tools should go in their cabinet or drawer, too. That might include a steady peeler, veggie chopper, spreader, melon-baller and an easily portable cutting board.

- Kitchen rags and a small dustpan/broom should be in an easily reached spot. If a spill happens, it's no big deal! "It's OK! The world isn't over. Here's how you clean it up… I'll help you."

- Invest in a sturdy step stool or "tower" so that your Asperkid can stand beside as a respected participant and help with food preparation, dishwashing, and so on.

- Eliminate countertops full of used glasses by providing a spot where family members can rest a glass that they will use again that day. (The one in the photo below is made of spray painted ceramic tiles from the craft store!)

PREPARE THE ASPERKID

The easiest thing to do is to forget how many variables and steps are involved in the most menial of tasks.

- Take your time when you teach new skills! Make sure that your Asperkid REALLY has the first step or two of a process mastered (with accompaniment and then independently) before you build on that foundation. Even a two-year-old Asperkid CAN prepare his own lunch (from getting supplies to using them correctly to putting everything away) given the right tools, instruction, and plenty of time to work.

- Demonstrate (from start to finish) everything you ask of your Asperkid.

- Be patient. It's going to take your Asperkid longer to shell peas, chop garlic, or crack an egg than if you did it yourself…but if we do everything ourselves (or worse, if we snatch jobs back from our Asperkids), the lesson we've taught is that he or she isn't "good" enough to meet our expectations. That's a lousy feeling, and one which an Asperkid will generalize to many other challenges. "If I can't do it perfectly," they will conclude, "why bother doing it at all?"

KEEPING THE BALANCE: CHOICE AND RESPONSIBILITY

- Don't be put off by a resistant Asperkid who hasn't been challenged like this before.

- Make *how* a task is done optional, not *whether* it's done. Example: "You are in charge of dishwashing. Would you like me to walk through the steps with you while you do them, or would you like to finish on your own?" Quitting because something is tough, tedious, or "bor-ring," however, is not up for discussion.

- If your Asperkid is to set the dinner table, ensure that he has the correct number of forks before he begins. If he ends up with an extra, somebody's missing a fork. If he runs short, he double-dealt! That's called "control of error." The materials themselves, rather than a scolding parent or teasing sibling, show when an adjustment is necessary and allow independent correction.

You can even draw and laminate placemats labeled to show the positioning of plates and utensils.

• Provide sensory feedback through gel seats, fidgets, and so on if your Asperkid needs help remaining at the table. You can even use a visual timer to show the time you require him or her remain there—even if they have to stand. By doing so, you teach that meals are social, not just utilitarian, experiences.

EXTEND THE SKILLS BEYOND THE FRONT DOOR

- Use meal time as a place to practice good manners and social skills. Teach your Asperkid to ask about others' days, and to listen well enough to ask a follow-up question.

- Expect spills. Expect goof-ups. Following the multi-task steps in recipes is HARD for these kiddos. That's OK. Model how to respond to "failure" without freaking out. What do you do when the cake is in the oven and you forgot to add the oil?! Improvize, and think outside the quadrilateral parallelogram (box)!

- Cooking is one of the first and most concrete ways of practicing fractions, comparing volumes versus weights, mixing solids and liquids, multiplying or dividing recipes, displaying hospitality (social skills) or philanthropy, playing with chemistry (why do egg yolks destroy a meringue?), learning abbreviations (e.g. that "lb." means "pounds") or how to convert American cookbooks to metric measurements, investigating family history or travel (through recipe exploration), getting messy (and cleaning up!), and experiencing

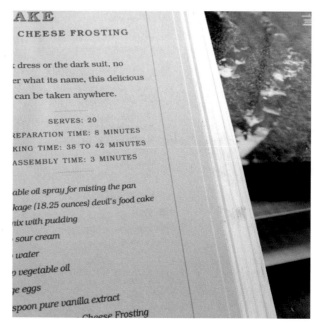

direct gratification for one's work…unless, of course, you forget the sugar or eggs and the cake flops. Even then, it's a great lesson in what happens when you miss a step in a sequence!

Wishy Washy

When electric dishwashers came onto the scene more than half a century ago, they were the darlings of every housewife who was lucky enough to own one. And certainly, as the busy mother of three, I love being able to push a button and know my day's worth of plates and pans are going to be sanitized while I head up to bed.

Yet only recently did I actually even learn that there *is* a correct way even to do *this* job (thank you, Martha!). So, while taking into account your own Asperkid's sensitivities to the sounds of clanking plates or the feel of slippery food bits (I have to admit that I have a terrible time with both), do explicitly show your Asperkid *how* to load the dishwasher for maximum efficiency (and less do-overs). Aspies, after all, like clear guidelines. Here are a few good ones:

Mechanics

Before loading those dishes, appeal to your Aspie's mechanical mind. Look to see whether there are two water distributors or only one, and where the water actually enters the washer. Also, remember to teach your Asperkid how and when to adjust the washing cycle, depending largely on what is in the dishwasher—a heavy-duty cycle for pots and pans, a gentle cycle with cooler water for anything fragile.

Don't Do It!

Wooden utensils and pans with wooden handles can be warped by the heat of a dishwasher—so keep them out! Hand-painted dishes, lead crystal, silver pieces, certain plastic pieces, and some glassware are not recommended for machine washing and may also need to be cleaned by hand (when in doubt, don't).

Scrape...

- Teach your Asperkid (from the get-go) to scrape off any large particles or caked-on food clumps.

- Believe it or not, dishwasher makers say that a little grime actually can help because it gives the soap something to cling to. So don't get too caught up with "pre-washing."

Bottoms Up

These points probably seems obvious to you, but they won't to your Asperkid who has probably never given much thought to "efficient dishwasher loading," and who may not be overly interested in preventing a chip or crack. So...

- Grab a home improvement book and actually poke around inside the washer to see which parts have which jobs and where they need to reach.

- Place cookie sheets, pans, and large platters along the outside of the bottom tray so that they do not block the rotation of the washing arm or the spray of the water.

- Do a little **show and tell**. Load a few pots, bowls, or pans facing up, and ask your Asperkid to predict what will happen if they are loaded that way. If he's not sure, toss some water on them and ask again (they'll fill up with dirty wash water and have to be cleaned over again!).

- Place plates, saucers, larger bowls, pots, and pans onto the rest of the bottom tray. Try to **stagger** the smaller plates and larger plates; this allows for better water flow between them.

You Say Cutlery, I Say Silverware...

Place all silverware *handles down*, except for knives, which should always be placed with their handles up. (See Appendix 3 on kitchen safety for more basics.)

Almost Done—The Top Shelf

- Load mugs, glasses, smaller bowls, and lids on the upper tray.

- Dishwasher-safe plastics belong up here, as well.

Lather Up

- Dishwasher techs will tell you that granule-type detergents (loose or in tablets) plus rinse agents are better at getting rid of stains and leaving glassware streak-free.

- Close and *lock* the door!

And that's all, folks! Well, until it's time to unload, anyway...

3...2...1... BLAST-OFF!
THE LAUNCH PAD

Visual schedules break down sequences, create a sense of independence, and keep kids on-task longer.

VELCRO TABS ALLOW KIDS TO MOVE TASKS TO THE "DONE" SPOT WHEN COMPLETE OR TO BE REWARDED FOR SUCCESSIVE COMPLETIONS WITH "STARS" TOWARD A LARGER PRIZE.

Organization is, generally, not an Asperkid's strong point. The same is likely true for time management. Let's be fair: if we Aspies are likely to get lost in the depths of our favorite book—or even pondering the shape of a cloud—getting anywhere on time is just not going to happen naturally. So whip out that label maker and get set to streamline your "departure zone." Calm and efficiency are not only possible (with discipline, effort, and planning), but from the moment your family enters the house, they are necessary.

Why? A cluttered, disorganized entryway ruins school mornings and creates unnecessary panic (such as discovering Mom was supposed to bake three dozen cupcakes last night). In what seems like an instant, shoes can migrate to the middle of the living room, book bags are left in the car and school notices end up in the road. Tempers flare, tears flood, and sometimes, someone shows up at school with one sneaker. Not good.

Between multiple extracurricular activities, various shoes in various sizes, ever-changing seasonal outerwear (from sunglasses to mittens), sports gear, backpacks, and stray library books, modern families have a lot of "stuff" to keep tamed—and often, that "stuff" has to be accessed or put away in a great hurry.

Hence, the need for the Launch Pad. It's the take-off and landing point—the buffer zone between home and everywhere else. The Launch Pad is where all of those rain boots and due-tomorrow school projects are sorted out for easy, predictable access. Regardless of specifics, you know your Launch Pad is a success if people can get in and out quickly, knowing where their belongings go, and where they will be when needed next. Once the area is set, gloves will be paired, lunch boxes emptied, and no one will show up to school shoeless… Usually.

PREPARE THE SPACE

- Walk through the experience. Where do your family members enter your home? Lower your vantage point to your kiddo's height (if appropriate) and see what he sees (or doesn't). Can he reach his coats or hat?

- Tame the insanity (not to mention the germ fest) of Shoes Gone Wild by leaving a shoe cubby and/or boot tray at the family entrance. Take 'em off/put 'em on as you pass by.

- Peg hooks (for sweaters, bags, etc.) are the easiest to manage, so Asperkids in a rush will have the most success with these. They're the last thing the kids use going out the door, and the first spot they reach when they come home.

- Provide one hook for each child's daily coat and one for her school bag; mount them where the family enters (in our case, they're actually in the garage). Remember to put hooks up for drying wet jackets or umbrellas.

- Contain the small stuff in baskets or shallow bins. Keep pairs of gloves, hats, and scarves sorted and accessible. Leave one basket for lonely mittens whose mates are missing.

- Teach your Asperkid to unpack any leftovers from their lunch box and put any dirty clothes straight into the laundry as soon as she comes inside.

- Hang large cork bulletin boards by the entrance, one designated for each kiddo. Use them to keep invitations and other time-sensitive materials in plain view. Be sure to remove items as dates pass.

- Asperkids have a notoriously tough time being aware of where their bodies are relative to other people (especially if that also involves figuring out where other people are trying to go). To eliminate "human traffic jams," something as simple as "X-marks-the-spot" in duct tape indicates where your Asperkid should sit to put on/remove shoes WITHOUT getting in everyone's way.

- Turn an old armoire or cabinet into an "extracurriculars locker." Sort gear into tote bags, one bag per kiddo, per activity— LABELED clearly. All of the totes go in the old armoire, and shut the craziness behind the cabinet doors.

PREPARE THE ASPERKID

- Time is an abstract concept for any child; it's particularly tough for kids with attention troubles. Visual timers (with or without sound) give your Asperkid a more "controlled" sense of passing time and help gauge how much time is left before a transition (like time to finish eating or to leave for school, etc.).

- Post a general schedule in a central location (use pictures for non-readers). Like all of us, Asperkids feel calmer and more prepared when they can see what the day has in store.

TIDYING UP

"Clean Up, Clean Up, Everybody, Everywhere. Clean Up, Clean Up. Everybody Do Your Share."

Carol Channing once recorded a spoken-word hit called "Housework." No matter how friendly and cheery the gal on television is while cleaning her toilet, Channing says, no matter how calm and affable that father is when he comes upon little Johnny scribbling all over the coffee table…they are laughing and smiling and cheering because (pregnant pause) they are actors. They are being paid real, actual money for talking about the wonders of the Magic Eraser or the fresh forest scent of Pine-Sol.

Doing the wash together may not make it "sunny," as Ms. Channing advises, but it does make it fair. And it does make each of us able to care for the most basic realities of our existence. We all make messes. The whole universe tends towards chaos, so should your house be any different? Yes, actually, because it has to be—for the sake of the Asperkid living there.

The Concentration-Building, Executive-Functioning Strengthening, Sense-of-Sequence Developing…"Not a Bunch of Chores" List

As adults, it's hard to remember (or even realize) that while we "work" to change something about our life or environment, growing minds and bodies engage in "work" (and play) to create change in *themselves*. Independence and self-reliance. Along with love and a stable environment, independence and self-reliance are a child's greatest needs—and direct indicators of how successfully they will function in life.

Grace and courtesy, care of oneself and of one's environment—these all begin by developing skills at home. And it gets better: while our kiddos practice sweeping up crumbs or hanging laundry, they are learning to see a task through from its beginning to its completion. They are honing hand/eye/muscle movement control that they will need for all types of learning tasks including writing and keyboarding. They are integrating order, outcome, and understanding into the beginnings of inner self-control, taking turns, delaying gratification, and extending attention spans.

So let me be clear: what follows are not "chores" to dole out. They are progressively complex, multi-step processes which you can teach as part of daily life in the kitchen, the bathroom, the laundry room, the bedroom. Your Asperkids will learn to become more self-sufficient, yes, but also (and maybe for the first time) truly eager to be independent of adult help. Gradually, you *will* become less important, and your Asperkid will become more and more in charge of his own life.

Super-Important REMINDER About the "Process"

1. Introduce all new tasks and materials through **demonstration, concentrating on your ACTIONS**, not on lots of explanation. Then let your Asperkid try, providing guidance only as needed!

2. **Repeat. And repeat. And repeat again.** Kids like to watch and read favorite shows and stories because multiple exposure leads to mastery. Your Asperkid will gradually recognize that the reason to do the work is not to get the approval of adults (aka "Look at me! Look at me!"), but to **succeed at a real task, through independent effort, and by her own thinking and judgment**.

EARLY TASKS (BY AGE THREE)

You'd be surprised how much even the youngest children can do when instructed patiently—and when adults don't "correct" hard work! Value effort over the product. Early tasks include:

- using simple carpentry tools

- putting materials away on the shelves where they belong when finished

- sweeping, vacuuming floors/rugs

- dusting, polishing floors, tables, silver

- carrying liquids without spilling

- walking without knocking into furniture or people

- carrying objects without dropping them ("thumbs on top, fingers underneath" is my mantra!)

- using scissors with good control

- dressing oneself: buttoning, zipping, snapping, buckling, bow tying, choosing seasonally appropriate (and very possibly mismatched!) outfits

- learning phone numbers

- pouring liquids without spilling (hand washing, watering plants, pouring during recipes)

- flower arranging

- using common household tools: tweezers, tongs, eye-droppers, locks, sponges, basters, spoons

- turning on taps/faucets safely

- caring for plants and animals (feeding, grooming, medicines)

- table setting, serving yourself and others; using appropriate table manners

- simple cooking and food preparation

- dishwashing

- weaving, bead stringing, etc.

- folding cloth: napkins, towels, etc.

- courtesy: eye contact (it's OK to look at the space between someone's eyes—they can't tell you're not making truly making eye contact!), shake hands with correct duration and pressure, make introductions, offer assistance, get the attention of someone engaged in a conversation

- simple use of needle and thread (gingham makes a great natural running stitch base).

PRACTICE USING THOSE "HOUSEHOLD" TOOLS (LIKE TONGS) BY MOVING MARBLES ONE BY ONE ONTO THE SUCTIONS CUPS AT THE BOTTOM OF BATH TREADS!

OLDER ASPERKIDS

Older Asperkids (from age six to late teens/early twenties) need to advance basic skills by integrating more complicated problem-solving challenges. For example, we have to explicitly teach:

- running one's own bath or shower (knowing how to safely adjust the temperature)

- washing and drying hair regularly

- care of one's own nails

- sewing (with a machine and patterns)

- cooking complex recipes; this includes clipping coupons, comparison shopping, assembling shopping lists

- working with tools and making simple home repairs

- caring for younger siblings

- running a home-based business enterprise (craft sales, computer repair, web design, babysitting, dog walking, shoveling, etc.) including budgeting, expenses, advertising, keeping commitments, and calculating and collecting fees

- gardening—designing "fairy gardens," landscape planning, purchasing, planting, cultivation, and harvesting.

Actually... I saw a poster once that read, "Actually, I can." And if there's one thing we all want our Asperkids to know, that may very well be it. Because whatever the challenge... actually, yes, they can. And this is how we show them.

PREPARE THE SPACE

- Rotate chores weekly so that no one tires of any one job. This week it's Recycling Officer (who clears, sorts, and brings out refuse), and next week it might be Animal Care or Kitchen Staff (responsible for wiping down tables, daily sweeping, and keeping paper towels stocked). Allow kids to bargain and trade if they wish.

- Make sure you walk through and demonstrate what each "job" entails, exactly where to find supplies, and (if applicable) when the job needs to be done. For example: "Bathroom Attendant check toilet tissue supply Mon/Thu, wipe counters with spray and paper towel daily."

- You can even create a checklist (in text or pictures) for your Asperkid to be sure he's finished all aspects of the task.

- Place a sturdy step stool in front of a top-load washer so shorter kiddos can reach and learn how to use the machines.

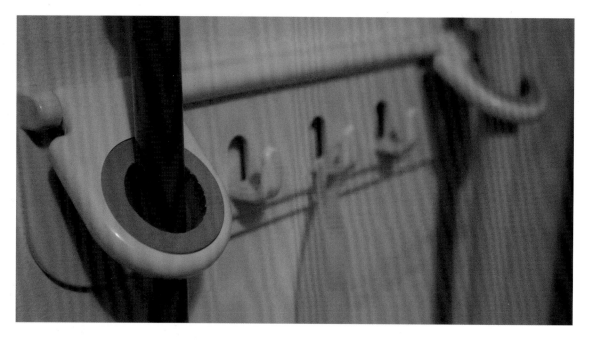

- Tools should be visually appealing, sized appropriately, available, and faithfully kept in the "their" designated places.

- Supplies need to be close to where they will be used—or they won't be used.

- Hang or place gear so that nothing has to be moved or is likely to be knocked over when your Asperkid gets or replaces his supplies.

WHAT'S ON THE LESSON PLAN? THE "I'M PART OF THE HOME TEAM" SKILLS YOUR ASPERKID NEEDS TO KNOW

1. Basic Sewing

- Put together a "practice tray" with a few choices of buttons, fabric, and thread.

- Teach your Asperkid to thread a needle (start with needle-threaders and large eyes at first; try floral foam for an easy pincushion), and to tie off the ends.

- Show how to do a basic running stitch and finish it.

- Demonstrate sewing on a replacement button (practice with different sizes).

2. Laundry Skills

- Sorting.

- Stain removal.

- Washing (going through the steps of hand washing and machine washing).

- Drying (teaching both line drying and the settings on a machine).

- Folding (include shirts, pants, socks, underwear—each of which require different techniques!).

A LOVELY WAY TO TEACH FOLDING (WHICH REQUIRES BILATERAL COORDINATION AND GOOD SPATIAL RELATIONS) IS TO DRAW OR STITCH "FOLD HERE" LINES ON OLD TOWELS, FOLDING INTO HALVES, THIRDS, AND QUARTERS.

3. General Housekeeping Skills

- Toilet scrubbing.

- Dusting.

- Sweeping (using various sorts and sizes of brooms).

- Crumbing tables.

- Wiping tables and countertops.

- Washing tubs, showers and sinks.

- Taking out the trash.

- Window washing.

- Polishing mirrors, glass, and silver.

POLISHING IS A GREAT EXERCISE IN CONCENTRATION, PATIENCE, AND MASTERY OF FINE MOTOR WORK. KEEP THE SUPPLIES TOGETHER: CLOTHS, WATER DROPPER, POLISH OR SOAP, EVEN A BASKET FOR SOILED BUFFERS. THEN, TEACH YOUR ASPERKID HOW TO USE THEM, AND LET "WORK" BE BOTH SATISFYING AND FUN!

A Brief (But Sweeping) Story

Do you remember when pictures had to be developed at a camera or convenience store, and your completed order contained strips of film negatives? For every "positive" printed out on photo paper, there was a color-reversed negative master copy in which light appeared dark and vice versa. Any future copies you'd wish to make required the negative.

Asperkids' minds work a little like that master copy—requiring both sides of a concept to master and recreate it. Recently, I practiced sweeping with my six-year-old. Because bilateral coordination is tricky for him (that's simultaneously using both hands to do different tasks, adding up to one composite task), managing both a dustpan and whisk broom together was proving more challenging than we'd anticipated.

Enter a classic lesson from Montessori education: the tape square on the floor.

First, I defined the target "sweep-up spot" with a masking-tape square on the kitchen floor. And then my Asperkid got to scatter buttons all around the perimeter.

"Where," I asked the instantly delighted spill-maker, "is the mess?" Of course, he told me that it was all over

the floor. After a few more questions, he was able to clarify; the buttons were all around the square (positive for mess), but the area inside the tape was empty (negative for mess). Nothing was spilt there. Alright, then: his goal for today, I explained, was to use the whisk broom to sweep the buttons into the "target zone" using as few passes as possible.

In short order, he discovered that carefree motions sent buttons flying; uncontrolled movements wrought sloppy results and more work. (And hey, we connected, wasn't that also true with penmanship? If you use frivolous strokes, the result is unclear—and usually means re-dos.) Instead, gentle, short strokes brought the buttons into place without overshooting and with much less work.

And then where were the buttons? Outside the square was now negative for spillage, he observed. Inside the square was now positive. He could tell he had successfully completed the task because he observed both a positive and a negative result…both of which can be seen in almost every circumstance. If you respond correctly in a social situation, you *do* get smiles (positive) and you *don't* make people uncomfortable.

The need for "both sides of the coin" is visible everywhere in Asperkid world—most especially in their language. This same kiddo will ask me, "Is everyone outside?" Upon hearing "yes," he'll follow up with, "So no one is inside?" He needs both an observable positive and negative to confirm that he is correctly interpreting the language and the social cues around him. Teach your Asperkid to assess completion in all things by finding both the positive and negative, or "lack of." Demonstrate it concretely at home via sweeping, cleaning the sink, pairing socks...and apply it to play dates, dating, even job interviews. These are, after all, your Asperkid's "master" images from which she will learn to independently make her own "copies" ever after.

Hang Ups

To keep the family laundry moving and coats off the floor, we have to use hangers; but like many other skills, hanging clothing is harder than you realize! Model and go slowly.

1. Lay shirt flat on the floor, front/design down.

2. Insert the corner of the hanger at the collar (from the bottom is just too tricky). Stretch the left side of the collar gently until the hanger slides in.

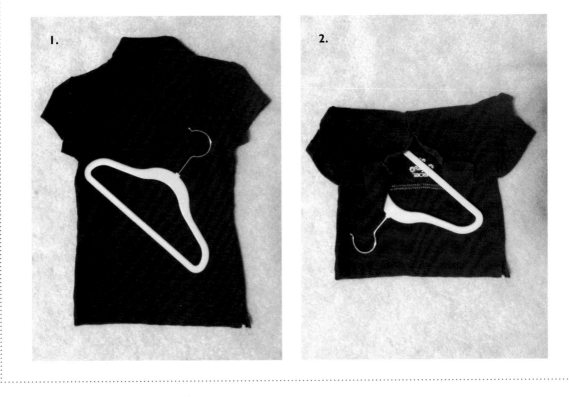

3. Do the same on the right side until only the hanger's hook is still visible.

4. Pick up the hook and shake the shirt gently so it settles. Hang it up in its proper place.

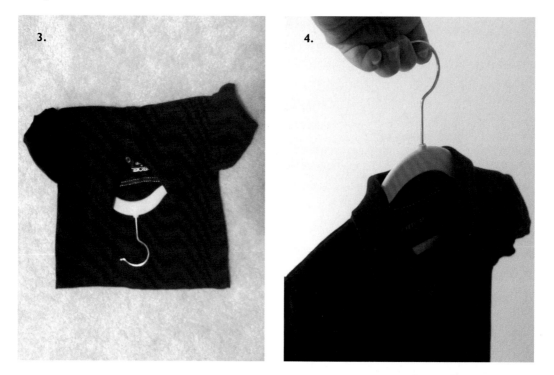

You can even start by doing three steps (then two, etc.) and allowing the Asperkid to finish, which guarantees some early success. And beware: pants hangers are a totally different lesson!

REMEMBER "MARY POPPINS" AND HER "LET'S TIDY UP THE NURSERY" GAME? THE RIGHT TOOLS (AND ATTITUDE) CAN MAKE EVEN MUNDANE JOBS FUN.

WE DISCOVERED THE FLIPFOLD ON *THE BIG BANG THEORY* AND FELL IN LOVE!

PREPARE THE ASPERKID

When you take the time to procure, place, and teach the use of appropriate tools, and when you can remember that task completion trumps perfection or speed, you are doing far more than sorting socks. You are teaching your child how to govern herself. You are modeling and instilling problem-solving and reasoning.

You are gifting your Asperkid an understanding of concrete skills so that she will learn, bit by bit, to independently resolve other, more abstract challenges.

KEEPING THE BALANCE: CHOICE AND RESPONSIBILITY

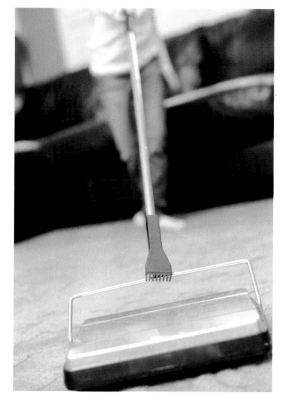

- Involve your Asperkid in choosing the scents of soaps or even in trying out homemade cleaning recipes. The more involved he is, the more invested he will be.

- Allow your Asperkid to pick what he wants to learn next whenever you can. Which shall it be, sewing on a button or folding sheets? (Notice "neither" is not an option.) Or, offer a choice of methods for completing a task: would he prefer to use the vacuum or carpet sweeper (both great proprioceptive heavy work, too!)?

EXTEND THE SKILLS BEYOND THE FRONT DOOR

- Sewing involves a lot of math. If you have a machine, let your Asperkid choose a pattern for a Halloween costume, a beanbag, whatever—then be sure he takes part in the measuring, cutting, and execution.

- Soap is alkaline. Why? What does that even mean? Using regular old litmus paper, run some chemistry experiments together to determine the pH of vinegar, dish soap, water, lemon juice, honey, and so on. And while you're at it, find out what pH stands for!

- Do you know how jeans were invented? Or who came up with the zipper? All people need clothing, but what we wear has a lot to do with historical events, science, cultural mores, religion, and geography. Explore the history of fashion online, in museums, or even through historical coloring books! Learn about how science has directly impacted the textiles we use today.

The Asperkid Versus the Advanced, Multi-Step Process of Table-Washing (No Contest: We've Got This)

Once your Asperkid has got the basics down, he's ready for more advanced multi-step processes; the method by which you demonstrate them, however, is just the same, and it's as important as ever to ensure that he's accomplishing meaningful activities with *real* materials that you've prepared ahead of time.

For example: here's a basket containing everything an Asperkid needs to independently wash a kitchen table *without* adult help—a soft-bristle brush, a sponge, a drying towel, a bowl to collect dirty water, a pitcher, and liquid soap. And yes, he *can* do this—but do take a good look at how complicated even "simple" housework can be…

1. The Asperkid retrieves the caddy/basket/tray containing his materials, and carries it to the table.

2. He removes any items—plants, condiments, placemats, and so on—from the table one at a time, placing them on a nearby counter.

3. He collects a table-crumbing brush, pan, or a cloth, and removes any large debris from the surface.

4. The crumbs or scraps are tossed in the trash, and the sweeping/crumbing tools are returned.

5. Then, he goes to the sink to fill the small pitcher with water to whatever "fill line" has been designated beforehand.

6. He carries it, slowly and carefully, to the table.

7. He lays out all his materials and then begins his work.

8. He pours a small amount of water onto the table, then adds a squirt of liquid soap.

9. Using the brush in circular motions, he distributes the soapy water, then scrubs the entire surface and legs thoroughly.

10. He dips the sponge into the pitcher and squeezes out all excess water.

11. He then wipes every surface that has been scrubbed, stopping occasionally to squeeze out any dirty water into the small bowl.

12. He then repeats the process until the entire table has been wiped down.

13. Then, he dries everything with the kitchen towel.

14. When done wiping with the towel, he wrings out the towel over the bowl at a low height.

15. He takes the soiled towel to the laundry, where he hangs it to dry or puts it into the washing machine, as directed.

16. He brings the brush and sponge to the sink, rinses both thoroughly under hot water and wrings ALL excess water from the sponge into the sink.

17. He carries the bowl of dirty water to the sink, pours it out gently and rinses it with clean water.

18. He brings the pitcher to the sink and pours out any remaining water.

19. Using a dry towel at the sink, he dries off the bowl and pitcher, and hangs the damp towel.

20. He places the sponge, bowl, pitcher, soap bottle, and brush back into the caddy, and replaces the carrier back in its designated spot.

21. He returns all items (centerpiece, placemats, etc.) back to their original places on the table.

PRIVATE SPACES AND QUIET PLACES

Bedrooms, Bathrooms, Study Spaces, and Small Spaces

Because of our trouble separating our own mind and knowledge from other people's, Aspies don't understand the concept of "privacy" particularly well. Moreover, the idea of public versus private space is completely unnatural—we can learn it, but we are, most definitely, *learning* (not innately knowing) why opening closed doors and drawers makes folks mad.

So if you find your Asperkid traipsing all over personal boundaries—walking in brazenly whilst siblings change clothes, thinking nothing of "borrowing" one another's possessions (without malice)—don't be surprised, or even very mad. First, offer clear, specific explanations of where and what you consider to be appropriate delineation between public and private spaces. (An easy tip we use is: "If a room has a door, it's a private place where private things happen or can be discussed; otherwise, it's public space and not the place for private topics or activities.")

Even then, impulsivity or compulsion may get the better of good decision-making. In that case, be patient and keep trying. And, if all else fails, here's a tongue-in-cheek suggestion for our visual-thinking, concrete reminder-loving Asperkids—straight from my own home where we literally sectioned off the house with police tape to mark: this is personal space. DO NOT ENTER without permission. This is a public space. DO NOT expect quiet or privacy here.

Sure, I'm positive we'll have to repeat the rules, but a point was definitely—and clearly—made. (And it was pretty funny, too!)

HOW TO CREATE A TRULY "DREAMY" BEDROOM

External order brings internal order. That means a physical place where everything is sized appropriately, attractive, and organized, and will maximize independence, self-confidence, and calm.

Why? As Asperkid families, we are constantly negotiating emotional roller-coasters, inattention, anxiety, and obsessive perfectionism. So your Asperkid's room has to be the antidote: an ordered haven where the worries of the world can be shut out. And, just as importantly, over which she can gradually exert independent mastery. Of course, the look of a child's room at age 3 versus age 13 will differ to some degree. Taste and decor may evolve from princesses to zebra print, or superheroes to…well, superheroes. Whatever the theme, the primary

job of the space remains: peaceful rest, easy dressing, daytime down-time…and, on occasion, escape from crazed siblings. Or parents. Or both.

A SOFT PLACE TO LAND

In the beloved children's classic, *Harold and the Purple Crayon*, Harold, a hero in footie-pajamas, draws himself an adventure…which is, after all, what our children are doing every day. They are creating themselves and the paths they will follow. When he finally gets tired, though, when he's had enough of drawing skyscrapers and oceans and mountains, Harold looks for "his" window into "his" room, finally climbing, with great satisfaction and comfort, into "his" bed.

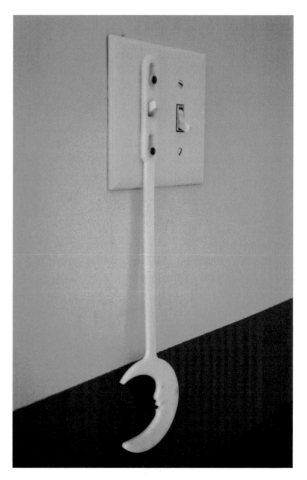

Our Asperkids are no different. Every child, whether toddler or teenager, needs to know that "his" space is always waiting…that, no matter what happens "out there," this room will always be his soft place to land.

PREPARE THE SPACE

- Accessibility—"Can your child reach?" Add a light-switch extender, a lightweight step stool and a full-length mirror to enable discovery and independence.

- Furniture height should match the user: low beds and dresser surfaces mean younger Asperkids can make their bed, and clean and adjust their belongings independently.

- Every bedroom needs a comfy reading spot—an armchair, a beanbag, a papasan, a loft.

- People DO judge (and pick up) books by their covers, kids and teens included. Look for places where you can keep several books forward-facing (whether by your rotation or your Asperkid's choice).

- Plate holders, spice shelves, and even rain gutters make fantastic "cover-showing" book-shelves.

- Prepare the storage space. If you can, hang it, don't fold it. In a drawer full of shirts, your Asperkid will only ever see the top one. If he's looking for the Darth Vader tee he's-sure-is-in-there-somewhere, he's just going to dig through and cause destruction worthy of the Dark Side.

COMPARTMENTALIZE!

- Compartmentalize small items on countertops and within drawers (pairs of pajamas, underwear, socks, bathing suits, fidgets, barrettes, or elastics) by using diamond-shaped organizers, small bowls, hermetic jars, drawer dividers, and plastic tubs. The logical structure will appeal to your Asperkid's proclivity for patterns, sorting, and classification.

DRAWER DIVIDERS

COMPARTMENT TRAYS AND ADHESIVE HOOKS

TRAYS AND BOWLS KEEP FURNITURE TOPS CLEAR

KITCHEN ORGANIZERS AND CHALKBOARD PAINT KEEP HAIR ACCESSORIES AND LEGO BITS ORGANIZED

- Chalkboard paint can make a framed-out space or the side of a bookcase functional. Vinyl decals add personality, but can change as special interests do.

- Add room to move around easily by replacing closet doors with curtains—they are easy to use, add color and make the smallest closet look ENORMOUS!

- Group clothing by type (skirts together, long-sleeves together, etc.) on reachable rods or use tension rods that can be adjusted as your child grows. And even in the closet, segment EVERYTHING with smaller containers.

PREPARE THE ASPERKID

- Personalize a visual organizer or Velcro chart to help propel your Asperkid through daily routines; this way he has a point of reference to check himself against before anyone else does. (Be sure to show some of your own to-do lists, otherwise he may feel embarrassed to need the reminder.)

- Be clear when you ask an Asperkid to tidy up his room. Specific directions ("Please put away any shoes that are on the floor" or "Hang up your clean laundry") communicate specific expectations and help break overwhelming tasks into doable pieces.

KEEPING THE BALANCE: CHOICE AND RESPONSIBILITY

- Allow your Asperkid to be part of the design process. What's most important to have? What one item MUST be present? What can go?

- Leave one surface completely empty and suggest to your Asperkid that he use it to display a select number of items; he can rotate them, but not go over the number you set—almost like a museum exhibit. This limits clutter and focuses attention on whichever special pieces—model airplanes, trophies, shells—he chooses to showcase.

- Keeping the room picked up is not optional. How and when you ask your Asperkid to tackle a particular task, however, is. So instead of, "Would you please clean up the trash, dishes, and other things that don't belong?" try, "Would you like to hang up the clean laundry or put away the odds and ends on the furniture tops?" The Asperkid has a choice— but a choice that you, as parent, control.

Stylin'—the Asperkid Way

From dressing to hair brushing, taking care of oneself involves a lot more mini-skills and steps than parents realize. Set your Asperkid up for success. Provide the careful instruction and accessible tools he needs to stay on-task longer, increase dexterity, and recheck sequential order if his attention shifts.

If any task involves **more than three steps, create a visual organizer** or checklist to help maintain action. Again, you may not realize it, but there are a LOT of little steps within, for example, a "morning routine"—and a lot of variables. What if the instructions don't mention the restroom and your Asperkid has to go? Our littlest had an accident because he didn't see a "use the potty" spot on his routine and wouldn't deviate from the "rules." What if there's no mention of taking off pajamas—or where they should go once removed? Expect piles on the floor. In other words: your chart HAS to be **specific** and **clear**, and for attention's sake, **VISUAL**. Here's an example:

| WAKE UP TURN OFF ALARM | GO TO THE BATHROOM (FOLLOW CHART THERE) | MAKE BED | PJS IN LAUNDRY BAG | PUT ON TODAY'S CLOTHES |

At first, walk your child through the routine. Next, simply read the steps aloud…Then, just be present but silent. Last, leave the room—check in and use a mild voice to call him back to focus if needed.

Tips and Tricks for Fostering Morning Independence

- Fill a hanging sweater holder with plastic tubs—each containing a choice of outfit (kind of like the "looks" paired in catalogs or shops).

- Include socks, jewelry and/or accessories in each tub.

- "Pack" a week's worth of clothing; let your Asperkid choose a different "bin" every day.

Getting Off On the Right Foot

Using a permanent marker, draw small dots on the inside edges of shoe soles. When the dots touch, the shoes are on the correct feet.

Stepping Over the Stumbling Blocks

Even the best-laid plans crumble when mechanics get in the way: don't let it happen!

- Practice opening and closing zippers, snaps, buttons, and tabs.

- Put together an "open and close" basket with as many different kinds of closures as you can imagine (twisting, clicking, pinching, pulling, clamping, etc.); hide little trinkets inside as rewards.

All Buttoned Up

Still not convinced that dressing is tough stuff? Just look at how many "mini-tasks" are involved in the simple job of doing up buttons (and yes, your Asperkid needs to learn them all):

1. Using index finger and thumb of dominant hand grasp right side of button.

2. Grip material near buttonhole (using "helper hand") with index finger on bottom, and thumb on top near button.

3. Pull material, buttonhole to left and button to right.

4. Twist button, so it is half way in, just "peeking." Release hands.

5. Change hands so that dominant hand is holding material nearest button, your index finger is on the tip and your thumb is on the bottom.

6. Grasp button with helper hand using index finger and thumb.

7. Fold back the material and the buttonhole to the right, at same time pulling button to the left.

8. Repeat steps for all remaining buttons. Then, check your work: Are the buttons through the holes? Are they through the correct holes? Are there any open flaps left after the last button has been fastened?

Making the Bed (Level 1)

Ask an Asperkid what the toughest job is in the bedroom, and most often the answer is "making the bed." But aesthetically, the bed is the star of the bedroom. Even if the rest of the room is a bit, ahem, less-than-Zen, a well-made bed creates a centerpiece—and an awfully appealing place to crash at the end of the day.

While trundle beds are beautiful and bunk beds are fun—your kiddo is not going to balance on a ladder and make hospital corners. Prepare the room with whatever he will need, demonstrate the entire process—then gradually reduce involvement, and check back in from time to time. Cheer effort rather than perfection, and take pride in a rumpled bed that was independently made—your Asperkid is showing you AND himself that yes, actually, I CAN do this—and a whole lot more.

- Place a sleeping bag or one big, fluffy comforter over a fitted sheet (forget the fussy flat sheet). One simple zip of the bag or flip of the top blanket, and the bed is officially "made."

- Floor mattresses, platforms, divans, futons, and day beds allow easy in/out maneuverability for young children and add a definite cool "lounge" factor for teens.

LOW BED + SLEEPING BAG TOPPER
= EASY MORNING CHORE

Making the Bed (Level 2): Fitted, Flat, Duvets, and Pillowcases

Once your Asperkid is ready to graduate from the sleeping-bag-on-top-of-the-bedding stage, go slowly and offer praise for effort; let's teach your Asperkid how to sort the sheets and dominate the duvet. It's time to make the bed!

Protect the mattress with a **cover**; you may also want to add an "egg carton," down, wool or memory foam topper.

The **Bottom Sheet**: In the US, the bottom sheet is almost always a fitted sheet (with elastic running around the corners); elsewhere that bottom sheet may be a flat sheet. So here are your options:

Using a Fitted Bottom Sheet

1. Lay the sheet on top of the mattress, decorated side up, matching the longer sides of the sheet to the longer sides of the bed.

2. Pull the fitted pocket over the upper right mattress corner.

3. Now, look diagonally across the bed to the bottom left corner. Fit the edge of the sheet around that corner.

4. Move over to the other side and pull the pocket down over the lower right corner of the bed.

5. Lift up the upper left corner of the mattress toward the center of the bed. Slip the final sheet corner pocket over this corner and let it fall flat. The mattress will now be covered with a taut bottom sheet.

Using a Flat Bottom Sheet and Making Hospital Corners
(This may be a two-person job until your Asperkid gets the hang of it.)

1. Stand with your Asperkid on one side, near the foot of the bed, and lay the sheet out on the bed.

2. Pick up the edge about 12 inches (30cm) from the end of the bed, and lift it up until the part of the sheet that's hanging down forms a rough triangle.

3. While you're holding the sheet up, have your Asperkid tuck the bottom corner of the triangle tightly under the mattress.

4. Now drop the corner you've been holding and tuck that tightly under the mattress—you should have a neat 45-degree fold (an angled "pocket").

5. Repeat at the opposite corners.

The **Top Sheet**: This is a TOTALLY OPTIONAL STEP (one we omit at our house—but here's your how-to, just in case):

1. Place the wide hem of the flat sheet at the top of the mattress, with the more-decorated side of the sheet facing down. Try to make sure that the lengths hanging off the bed's longer sides are even.

2. Spread the sheet out evenly across the bed, allowing any extra length to fall at the bottom edge.

3. Follow directions above for making "hospital" corners at the foot of the bed only.

4. Tuck the remaining part of the flat sheet along both sides of the bed. My father-in-law (a former colonel in the US Marines) reminds me that for fun, you can check the "tucking" by bouncing a coin (or trying to, anyway!) in the middle of the bed.

Blankets: Show your Asperkid how to shake out and lay blankets atop the sheets.

1. Place blankets right-side up with the top of the blanket at the point where you turn down the top sheet, about 8 inches (20cm) from the top of the bed.

2. Tuck in the bottom edge and make hospital corners there.

3. Fold down the top sheet over the top edge of the blanket. Now the good side of the sheet is showing.

Top with a **comforter or duvet** spread out evenly over the bed. Run your hands across the middle, removing any wrinkles or creases.

Shimmy the **pillowcases** onto pillows with the tagged edge of the pillow going in first. Fluff and put them at the top of the bed.

Weighted Blankets: Some folks on the spectrum love the rest they get beneath the pressure of weighted blankets, which are available through occupational therapy catalogs or online craft sites like etsy.com. Other people don't like the heaviness at all, and kick everything right off.

In this case, as in most, if you've met one Asperkid, you've met one Asperkid. What works for one person won't necessarily work for everyone, but it's always worth a try (choose one that weighs about 10 percent of your Asperkid's body weight, plus 2 pounds/about 1kg).

EXTEND THE SKILLS BEYOND THE FRONT DOOR

- Wall decor is a creative…um, sneaky…um, clever place to reflect your Asperkid's interests, not to mention the subjects about which you'd like him to *become* interested.

- At your Asperkid's eye-level, hang framed prints of beautiful photographs and artwork. Maybe your budding oceanographer would find untapped inspiration in the majestic movement of "The Great Wave off Kanagawa," that famous 19th-century Japanese painting. Or perhaps your fantasy movie lover would be transported by the glamour of old Hollywood and become interested in photography. Ask for a chosen topic, then structure an associated infusion of aesthetic discovery.

Sweet Dreams

Your Asperkid's room is entirely about your Asperkid's feelings of security, ease of movement, and her self-care development. Don't worry about loftier purposes or fancier pillow shams. The real goals are large enough to *be* enough.

Concentrate on creating order, beauty, and simplicity. By building open spaces that feature quality over quantity, you teach your Asperkid that the value of everything—relationships, friendships, jobs, life—comes from usefulness and natural fit, not from abundance or sparkle.

SPLISH, SPLASH! I WAS TAKING A BATH (OR A SHOWER—WHICHEVER WORKS)

The restroom is one of the most frequently used spots in any home; it's kind of a public space that is privately used. This means that your Asperkid has to learn to master bathroom activities independently, but also understand the expectations others will have of each user: things will be left as they are found, wetness will be wiped, soiled clothing will be disposed of properly, seats will be closed, air filters will be turned on in certain situations, and so on.

As everywhere else, preparation of the space makes the process of developing concentration, curiosity, and confidence possible. The prepared space begets the process that begets the prepared, positive Asperkid. Be specific. Be clear. Be discreet. Whether you have a whirlpool tub or a shower stall is less important than whether the room enables your Asperkid to work toward independence and a sense of dignity.

SENSORY PRAGMATICS

Much of what parents can experience as "bathroom behavior problems" are really sensory sensitivities and sequencing trouble. One of the hardest realities to communicate to those who don't suffer sensory defensiveness is how truly painful and anxiety-producing the experience is. This is worse than nails-on-a-chalkboard bad. Your Asperkid is *not* trying to be difficult. She's trying to avoid pain.

For example, if a toilet's flush is too bothersome, your Asperkid may "choose to forget" to flush to avoid physical discomfort. Or perhaps the child's feet dangle when seated, making using the bathroom frightening. And if she's busy worrying about all the steps involved in turning on a light (assuming it's been made reachable), undressing, getting onto the toilet, cleaning herself, redressing, flushing, and hand-washing, she may not "make it" in time.

Similarly, if the sound of the bath water running feels "piercing" or rinsing out shampoo

really feels like drowning, no amount of logic is going to change that: your child IS going to resist the experience. After all, wouldn't you? That's why whenever addressing behavior issues in the bathroom, please, please be aware of the very real sensory, cognitive, and mechanical factors that may contribute to the trouble.

PREPARE THE SPACE

- A built-in step or a moveable stool makes the sink and toilet accessible without adult involvement; that means self-sufficiency and self-respect.

- Towels, replacement toilet paper, extra shampoo, and so on should be stored where everyone can reach them. Asperkids can't clean up after themselves if they physically can't complete the task!

- Anxiety is controlled by giving Asperkids some legitimate form of control. Provide a light plastic pitcher to tame the hair-rinsing drama. Plastic visors help, too.

- Using a permanent marker, label a plastic cup or bath caddy for each child. Each "named" cup or caddy holds a toothpaste pump, a differently colored toothbrush, and, ideally, a small cloth to dry the counter/sink.

- Organize cabinets and drawers by grouping like items in structured containers. Talk with your Asperkid about *why* items are grouped together, and try to get him to explain the sorting process in his own words. Consistencies and contrasts can be tough for even the smartest Asperkid to explain because his own impressions of things just seem "obvious."

PREPARE THE ASPERKID

"Hygiene" is a dirty word to most Asperkids. By nature, your Asperkid is not aware of (or interested in) the offense left by personal "scraps" (whiskers, soiled tissues, cut nails, etc.). Those are social expectations which you will need to spell out blatantly— along with the consequences of breaking those rules (health problems, annoyed roommates, even job loss). And do be the one to bring up everything from deodorant to acne lotion. As adults, it's our job to prevent these kids from "getting it" too late—after they've already been teased.

From the very beginning, the bathroom is a place to get over your own inhibitions and clearly model every step of every independent self-care skill your Asperkid needs to master (how and when to get a towel—which kind; how to turn on the water and what needs to be done with a shower curtain when water is running, etc.). It's important, therefore, to establish a

regular schedule of when your Asperkid must wash what parts of herself—an unarguable, clearly spelled-out self-care routine that includes bathing, combing, tweezing, shaving, and deodorants (when appropriate), feminine hygiene, tooth brushing/flossing, and what to do with the remnants of any of these processes.

A LITTLE BIT STUCK

While you demonstrate those slow, simplified steps, your Asperkid *will* become distracted. It might be hyper-focus on pouring out exactly the right amount of shampoo—is that too much? too little? do I rinse and repeat? It might be the act of squeezing and twisting wet hair. Expect a staccato-brand of learning, and you won't feel so frustrated.

EXTEND THE SKILLS BEYOND THE FRONT DOOR

Did you know that you can write on mirrored surfaces with dry erase markers, and wipe them clean easily with glass cleaner and paper towels? Once you've got the mirror in a place that your Asperkid can see clearly (and explained that she can ONLY write on the mirror and ONLY if you've given permission), use it as a surface for doing math equations, two-dimensional geometry, and even cartoons. The vertical surface is a good challenge for hand muscles, besides being a whole lot of fun.

A FEW MORE INCENTIVES

- Beyond the obvious comparisons of hot/cold, wet/dry, bathroom water-play is a fantastic playground of sensory experiences. There can be experiments in volume, cause and effect, and physics (Will it float? Will it sink?).

- The tub is also a super place for science experiments—while wearing bathing suits! It may be the middle of winter, but you can have a "state of matter" beach party experimenting with water as a liquid, solid (ice), and vapor (steam).

- If it sounds gross, kids love it, right? So, let your Asperkid use a toothpick to scrape the plaque off his teeth or tongue one morning, then wipe it onto a slide. Slip the glass under a microscope and see what's really growing in there (if that doesn't make them want to brush, nothing will).

- Fill the bathtub with water… and then jazz it up. Add plastic "glow sticks" and bracelets (the kind given as favors or at parties. You can have a glow in the dark party and even fill glasses with different colors, creating a "music of the night" xylophone. Can your child sing back the pitch or repeat the pattern you play?

STUDY SPACES

Many of our Asperkids, while amazingly bright or even brilliant, also struggle with hyperactivity, distractibility, dysgraphia, sensory concerns, organizational difficulties, visual processing problems, and learning disabilities. Your Asperkid's academic success and, more importantly, her self-concept as "smart" or "stupid" are at stake. Give her a fighting chance by finding a quiet, well-lit place where busy siblings and playful pets aren't vying for her attention; where you show her how to color-code, schedule study time, and highlight due dates. And remember: when you design your Asperkid's study space, you are literally setting up his or her work skills for life.

After all, a beautifully written, completely crumpled, day-late essay is not going to get good marks—nor will the taxman care why a payment is late. The real world doesn't often give do-overs. And we are preparing our precious Asperkids for a very real world.

PREPARE THE SPACE, PREPARE THE ASPERKID

- Keep homework logs in a central, public place—like on the refrigerator so that they are easy to see and attend to regularly.

- Break down weekly assignments with your Asperkid so she can get an idea of all the "mini-tasks" involved and leave adequate time for each.

- A visual timer can help kids stay on-task more efficiently.

- Remember: this is a work space. Prized collections, toys, and treasures belong someplace where they won't be a distraction.

- Install a "mail" box where your Asperkid can leave notices from school and you can return permission slips, lunch money, or teacher notes.

- Keep extra supplies stocked and predictably stored to prevent last-minute panic.

- Address sensory distractions. Provide noise-canceling headphones, restful things to gaze at to give eyes a break, sugarless gum, a quiet space, and really good (ideally, natural) light.

FIDGETS: SOME ASPERKIDS LITERALLY CANNOT CONCENTRATE *WITHOUT* THEM. KEEP A READY SUPPLY ON HAND.

SMALL PLACES

THE COCOON

Open spaces are exhilarating; they can also be busy, bright, and loud. When we are exposed, we are free—but, to a degree, we are also vulnerable. As human beings, we all need a sense of confinement to some degree. That's especially true for Asperkids, who live in a world that frequently feels chaotic, unpredictable, and scary. Within small, carefully constructed spaces, though, Asperkids can recharge, shut out the extra noise, the people, the touches, and the lights. They can feel safe enough to relax and to consider a big world full of big ideas, big feelings, and big experiences.

PREPARE THE SPACE

The "hideaway" requirements are really simple: a small area that is independently accessible, has soft textiles, controllable volume, adjustable lighting, and is free of clutter.

Build a "treehouse," or a nook under the stairs. A tent or swing outside. The particulars of the space that you use don't matter; what counts is the control your Asperkid has over it. In our home, for example, we turned a storage area into an indoor "treehouse"— which quickly became known as "The Thinking Room." There are bookshelves nestled into a nook and a snuggly rug for burrowing toes. A small, covered mattress strewn with throw pillows acts as a lounge spot, and a basket next to it is filled with fluffy blankets.

THE THINKING ROOM

PREPARE THE ASPERKID

The best part of "The Thinking Room" is the "Calming Jars." They're just glass canning jars, which each Asperkid filled to the brim with water and his or her choice of food coloring, glitter, and LOTS of glitter glue. Once tightly closed, the jars can be shaken, rolled, or simply tipped over—creating collisions of movement and shimmering color. After about five minutes, the motion finally calms and then settles. And so does the Asperkid.

THE "CALMING JARS"

Sometimes we all need to walk away and recenter. That's hard to do when you are upset, though. It's a skill that has to be taught before it is needed. And then, it probably has to be retaught when needed. And even then, you'll need to revisit and re-examine the experience afterwards. Knowing what you need emotionally and being able (and willing) to get it for yourself is no different than learning to satisfy a physical need—like getting yourself a drink when you're thirsty. Both are important for daily living. Both skills must be taught. And both take work to master.

Practice these important steps with your Asperkid:

1. Learn to recognize and identify frustration, boredom, anxiety. Where do you feel it in your body? Pay attention so you can recognize it in the future.

2. Ask yourself, "What will alleviate (fix) the feeling?" A drink? A nap? A fidget or alone time? A reassurance or even a hug?

3. Now go and get what you need—juice, a book, some time to think. (Your "designer" job is to make sure the space is always accessible!)

Don't forget to recognize your own need for quiet and respect it—especially when you feel overwhelmed or upset. Reference your choice in a later conversation with your Asperkid, and congratulate him when he follows suit.

KEEPING THE BALANCE: CHOICE AND RESPONSIBILITY

Offer retreat when you see your Asperkid needs it—but don't order her there. This is NOT meant as a "time out" or punishment. It's a positive recharging station that she can use, or not, as she likes. Instead, respect the space. Leave your Asperkid alone in there. If you want to talk, ask his or her permission to enter (remember: it's intentionally *not* your area to control).

EXTEND THE SKILLS BEYOND THE FRONT DOOR

- Purposely stock the space with books and objects your Asperkid might not otherwise take the time to examine: a geode, a flowering plant, a sand-and-water sculpture.

- Include a clock. Asperkids can get lost in their own worlds; they need some frame of reference as to how long they are "away."

- Experiment with introducing new "baskets" into the space that provide untested "escape" activities—you might include stitchery, a journal or sketch pad, an audiobook, crossword puzzles, or a Newton's Cradle.

- Inspire curiosity and conversations with prints of famous paintings or photographs.

PERSONAL SPACE

Alone time doesn't solve problems. It doesn't fix hurt feelings or explain social mishaps. Alone time does provide physical and psychological distance, personal reflection, and anxiety relief.

Given some time to unwind, Asperkids are much more apt to have rational discussions, consider compromises, and listen to others' perspectives. So will Mom and Dad. After all, sometimes all anyone really needs is a little "personal space."

Generalizing Instructions from Task to Task… aka What to Do Instead of Saying, "But I Already Explained That in the Bathroom!"

As your Asperkid gets proficient with processes around the house, fewer reminders and cues may be needed—or not. Sequences are tough. If your Asperkid knows how to do a task but just can't remember all of the steps, help him be successful. Write out bullet points on index cards (e.g. "Replace chairs under the table after sweeping"); laminate them for durability, and store them in a recipe box or photo album for easy access. It's also helpful to provide a visual timer and a rough idea of how long the task should take.

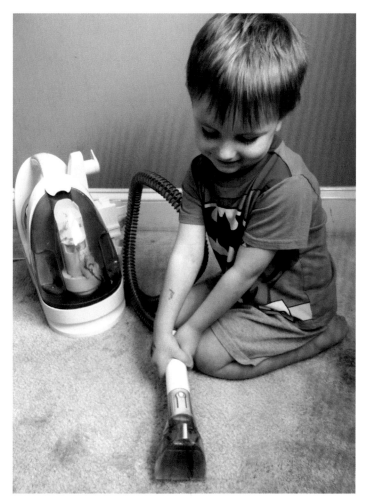

Do remember that generalizing doesn't come easily—so even if you explain that the bathroom countertop has to be cleared off before it can be cleaned, you may still have to make the same point in the kitchen. Your Asperkid *is* paying attention, but unless you make the connection aloud, the processes will likely remain distinct in her mind.

Whatever the task, praise the process rather than the product. After all, we're really teaching independence, perseverance, and follow-through—not perfect polishing. Other tricky jobs you may want to practice demonstrating:

- pairing socks

- cleaning out trash cans and putting new liners inside

- spot removal (from carpets, different types of materials, etc.)

- how to react to various kinds of spills—and WHEN!

- cleaning out traps in drains, dishwasher, sinks, and disposals

- folding towels and fitted sheets

- safely disinfecting with bleach.

AND OUT THE BACK DOOR

Outside Places

Asperkids' emotional security evolves from a certainty in their own physical security... especially in the richest (and thus, most intimidating) of sensory environments—the outdoors.

The outdoors is the most sensory-filled, great wide "somewhere" we can access, full of gross motor challenges, never-ending messes, and stinging bugs. It's also usually where the least-structured play occurs, and for Asperkids, that means negotiating changing social scenes, experimenting with being a leader versus being a boss, learning how to follow and play along, incorporating others' ideas… the tough stuff. I once heard that if you ask an adult to sketch out his favorite childhood memory, most often, those scenes take place outdoors.

Catching fireflies, building snow forts, snatching at slimy salamanders. While it may take your supportive, *patient* encouragement at first, getting Asperkids outside can help them feel more connected and less stressed. Their respect for physical labor and community involvement grows, and their sleep and cross-curricular, critical thinking skills improve. Best of all, increased sensory security begets creativity, adventure, and a humbling sense of purpose and awe.

With planning and a little humor, the outside world may be the most potent "room" of an Asperkid's home. It's limitless, it's free. And in every unexplored nook and cranny, it inspires the whispered words, "I wonder…"

Sean

Maura

PREPARE THE SPACE

- Accessibility—can your Asperkid get outside and be outside with some degree of privacy, safely?

- Are properly sized tools (gardening gloves, rake, clippers, pails, shovels, compost bin, watering can and spigot) available and displayed so that the Asperkid can plan what he needs, access whatever he needs, and then be able to return them independently?

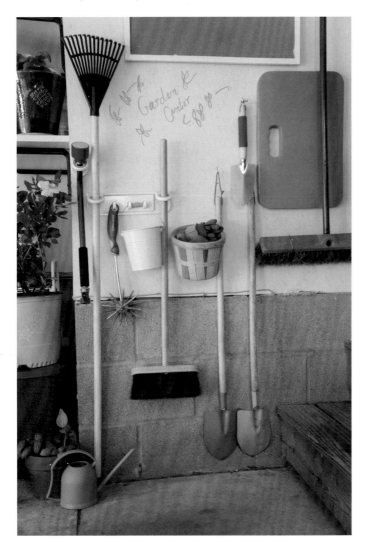

- Is there space for free-for-all digging? worm searches? leaf hunts? hands in the mud? If your Asperkid wants to go off and just make a mess, are tools available?

- Make a variety of activities possible—when your Asperkid needs sensory input to get calm, can she get to a swing, a scooter, a trampoline, a hopper ball, some rocks or a tree to climb? What about a hammock (with a step stool, if needed) for relaxing movement, or shoveling snow, sweeping pathways, mowing the lawn, hammering nails into boards, raking leaves, or pulling a long hose for proprioceptive (joint and muscle) input?

- Digging in sand or soil, carrying mulch in a wheelbarrow, or transferring water all give the heavy work Asperkids need to help overcome sensory defensiveness.

- Walking over uneven surfaces or climbing rocks pushes Asperkids to develop confidence in their movement and improves motor planning as they move from one surface to another.

- Don't undersell beauty. Make your outdoor space lovely—life is enriched by music and art… Why not by fragrant peonies, found-stone walls, cut-flower gardens, or waving ferns?

PREPARE THE ASPERKID

- Be present when you are present. Ditch the smartphone for a while. And expect to do more work than the Asperkid—at least at first.

- Go at your Asperkid's pace. Aim for participation not perfection. A crooked row of lovingly planted flowers is far more important than the neighborhood garden award.

- Asperkids crave context—how can outside exploration and work be connected with an Asperkid's natural love of facts? Can you dissect a flower and match its parts with a botanical puzzle? Or prepare a seasonal recipe from the garden harvest? Can she learn to cut and arrange flowers using some basic tools or experiment with soil pH, and its effects on flower color?

- Make comparative leaf rubbings, then learn about plant cells versus animal cells, monocots versus dicots, annuals versus perennials.

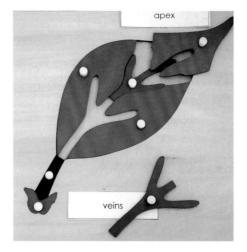

- Or find out why poison ivy makes us itch, how various bugs are helpful and/or destructive to agriculture, or what minerals are present in the rocks in your yard.

KEEPING THE BALANCE: CHOICE AND RESPONSIBILITY

- Give choice wherever possible, but have some activity to suggest to help engage your Asperkid. Does your Asperkid want to help design, purchase supplies for, and construct a bean tepee or a sunflower garden? Should the bendable willow or dogwood twigs become a sculpture or a trellis? Which kinds of birds would he prefer to attract to the space, and what feed will help to do that? Should we sketch, plan, and build a lookout, a stage, or a picnic table? Which vegetables should we plant?

- Try creating mini-settings around your property that vary in layout, intent, and exposure, so that your Asperkid could, for example, tend to a garden, play with bubbles, make homemade chalk, retreat to read in a hammock, and finally gather wildflowers for a dinner centerpiece.

- Ask, "What do *you* want to explore?" Let your Asperkid direct the experience.

EXTEND THE SKILLS BEYOND THE FRONT DOOR

- Make a sundial out of a straw and clay and practice measuring the angle of the sun using a protractor, then read about the history of time-keeping, calendars, and how ancient deities still show up in modern month and day names.

- Have an outdoor words scavenger hunt (write ON the actual objects in chalk and have younger kids find and trace the letters—e.g. sandbox, tree, slide).

• Make a giant hundred board out of chalk and jump to solve algebraic equations or basic skip counting patterns.

- Investigate photosynthesis as you dissect leaves.

- Use a flower press to create gifts for family, teachers, and friends.

- Have your Asperkid build strength and coordination using a wheelbarrow to haul the dirt for the garden, sand for the playground, or rocks for the pathway.

- Practice using a compass while investigating the Earth's magnetic poles and how they protect us from solar winds.

- Observe and draw the phases of the moon.

- Catch and identify the animals, plants, and insects in a pond.

- Experiment with rock salt and figure out why it melts ice in the drive.

- Top an egg carton with photos of items to find in the yard.

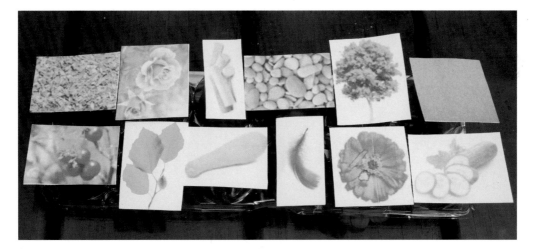

- Take photographs of garden life and turn them into Bingo, memory games or even homemade greeting cards.

- Learn about the life cycles of trees, frogs, butterflies, or apples.

- Build a potato clock.

- Dig out and maintain a fish pond.

- Construct a swing out of a recycled tire.

- Raise and sell produce or homemade jams/jellies/fruit or veggie breads at a farmers' market.

- Mend a fence and paint it—practicing measuring all along; learn to use a power drill and insert marbles into fence posts or gates to catch the sunlight.

- Create homemade perfumes and oils from cut flowers.

- Sketch out constellations as they change through the seasons and learn the myths that accompany them.

- Walk the family pet and observe what animals' "body language" communicates.

- Build a bird feeder, bird bath, or ladybug house.

- Set up an "ant farm" and bring some outdoor observations inside.

- Use nature rubbing plates and stencils to color and assemble a larger mural.

- Investigate worm anatomy and composting techniques; try creating your own compost kit then find out about decomposition, and what chemicals are released.

- Build a miniature garden out of mosses, pebbles, and dollhouse or craft supplies— get as elaborate as you can!

- Plant a butterfly garden and use guides to identify the visitors.

- Play in the rain (and find out what barometric pressure is while you're at it)!

- Observe a honeycomb—can you figure out why the shape bees use is the most perfect of all for structural support? (Hint: try building a tessellation!)

- What other shapes seem to reoccur in nature? Think of whirlpools and galaxies, shells and tornadoes. What about symmetry—where is it evident in animals? Insects? Plants?

- Dig in the dirt—find out which plants need which kinds of soil and why—and make yourself a fresh salad that you've planted, tended, and harvested yourself!

- Get MESSY! Make homemade sidewalk paint (it's just food coloring and cornstarch) and see what colorful creativity you can add to the great outdoors.

PART 2

THE PROCESS

OF "BECOMING" THE PEOPLE THEY ARE MEANT TO BE

Can you remember, if you think back, a time when you were in your "zone"? When you were able to calmly and entirely devote yourself to a task in mind and body… to lose yourself in an afternoon nap, finish the last chapter of that book you've always wanted to read, climb to the top of the high dive, plant a bed of flowers, or hear the last chorus of the song that always makes you cry…or sing…or dance? When you felt utter delight and concentration and absorption in the task at hand—to savor those last drops of an entire cup of coffee—and no one wrested you from it?

Those are complete moments. Whole, unbroken. And in those moments, you are able to be fully, totally engaged. You are the most alive you may ever be. Your mind is keen, your senses are attuned. You are drinking in the best the world has to offer and, just as important, readied to give back inspired ideas that only you can provide. You are, as Dr. Seuss might say, your "you-iest you."

Now imagine yours is an Aspie mind. Like your Asperkid's—like mine. We, Aspies, are easily distracted, bombarded by sensory input, derailed by the unimportant from the very momentum that had first carried us forward. Finding our "zones" can be tough. And we don't want to leave once we're there.

Take a second look at the Asperkid who is concentrating on zippering his jacket while trying to remember to go back for the bit of homework he left upstairs, while you chide him for leaving his breakfast dishes on the table, while his sister walks by shouting about finding her shoes, while the dog is barking to be let out and "Hustle! Hustle! Hustle!" someone yells. "It's time to go or everyone will be late!"

OK. Now stop. What are the odds of him remembering that homework? Or of retrieving it without knocking into his sister, snapping back at you, spilling the breakfast dishes while leaving the milk out, and putting it into the right homework folder in his school bag? This is not the launch pad of a child who must be brave as a superhero most every day. It's a maelstrom of physical and material chaos which begets broken relationships, dampened self-esteem, and unmet potential. It's kryptonite. In all our hurry, there is no space to breathe. No space to rest. Everything has to be right, and it has to be right now. But that's not really how the world works. A flower takes time to bloom. A person takes even more time to "become."

Pediatrician and educator Dr. Maria Montessori was the first to describe the importance of carefully structuring predictable spaces. She observed that, without fail, ordered spaces fostered physical and emotional security, and thereby encouraged independence in even the most broken of children. Put simply, these spaces, these places—the ordered, "prepared" environment—enabled the process of "becoming" whole, confident, peaceful, happy people.

When a young person—Asperkid or not—has the freedom and time to learn to take care of himself and to make mistakes and discoveries along the way, "practical" skills become much more profound. Coordination, concentration, and independence can be achieved through the comfortable repetition of simply squeezing juice, folding socks, hammering nails, washing dishes, or caring for plant life. It doesn't need to be any more complicated than that.

For an Asperkid to tap into whatever individual, unique gifts she was meant to bring into this world, she's got to come home to a place where she can learn to trust her own powers. Hooks and trays, dust brooms, and daily activity charts: these are the tools of everyday superheroes—not spandex-wearing crime-stoppers. Just brave, honest, loyal

children. And to become those "superheroes," they need a thoughtfully prepared place for the process to happen: a predictable, encouraging, and safe place. Our Asperkids will develop their lasting notions of independence, safety, self-worth, respect, and joy based upon the "home bases" we design. Those bases are the "places" where the "process" of becoming their best selves will happen. Or it won't.

Home is where your Asperkid's legend starts. It's the impetus for everything to come: whomever she goes on to love, wherever he longs to travel, whatever she seeks to discover, why he cares (or doesn't) about the world around him. That's where you come in as chief "designer," mentor, unconditional fan. You are the superheroes' first superhero, creating a protective space—a warm place—where the process of exploration is safe, where repetition is encouraged, where passive observation and active manipulation are all "good things."

Give them time to finish an idea. To make a mistake, make a mess, and then make it all over again. Then, watch them bloom—watch as they "become" the "superheroes" they are meant to be… a little bit more… every day. Give them the physical space they need to understand who they are, why they matter, and what they really can do.

The beginning…

PART 3

APPENDICES

PRESENTATION IS EVERYTHING

External organization nurtures every child's innate sense of order. Asperkids, in particular, rely on that order longer and more intensely because it allows them to successfully anticipate and establish an inner sense of control over their environment.

That's why how you display the items you've chosen for your home is almost as important as what you present. Visual grouping creates an organized calm—a "predictable" place for everything.

TRAYS

Whether fiberglass, melamine, Lucite, silver, or wood-grain, the weight of the tray should reflect the importance of the items it bears. Choose plastic for wet or messy activities, compartmentalized for clarity in sorting, and clear to eliminate competition with multi-colored materials. Raised edges help prevent slipping, shine beckons attention, handles are useful for larger loads. Even letter holders can display small photos and keep grouped books upright. Flower pot saucers work as jewelry holders next to bathroom sinks, easy earring corrals, or night-time holders for a watch or iPod.

CONTAINERS/BOXES

Choose clear acrylic to show off the contents, hand-carved wood or stone for alluring lines, nesting for space-saving, with drawers for accessibility or even color-coded to stay organized.

Pay attention to depth and size versus the objects inside so items stay put and in view. Even terracotta flower pots or unused paint cans (from craft stores) make pretty, functional containers for everything from chalk or crayons to paintbrushes or modeling tools, Lego bricks, or building blocks.

BASKETS

The natural, woven fibers in basketry are an art unto themselves. Small baskets are perfect for craft materials, beads, buttons, or marbles. Narrow, walled baskets complement dowels for woodworking, bundle colored pencils, or divide silverware.

Larger "totable" baskets with sturdy handles make collecting wildflowers more fun and harvesting the garden a joy.

THE CURIOUS INCIDENT OF THE FROG PRINT ON THE CEILING

Last year, we repainted our entire kitchen and living room. From Sunday dinners to family game nights, these are the spots where we spend most of our "together" time (even if "together" sometimes means side-by-side parallel play). And just by the nature of our floor plan, they are also among the first rooms guests see.

In other words, the update was important both because of what the rooms meant to our family, and also because of their public prominence. Let's face it. We all want our homes to meet our needs; we also want everything to look pretty when the in-laws come to dinner.

And ours really did. After lots of input from a dear friend with oodles of decorating talent and after several coats of paint, the place was (and still is) truly beautiful. Soft grey walls anchored in clean white bottoms, black-and-white decorator contrasts, and everything bordered by fresh white ceilings, chair rails, and trim. Just formal enough, just casual enough, just classic enough.

Just perfect. Mission complete.

About a week later, in a completely unconnected event, my mother happened to buy my middle son a rubber frog. You know the type, no doubt—one of those sticky things that you hurl at a wall and then watch it tumble down. Relatively harmless. But, being a five-year-old boy, my son was not content to watch his frog fall happily down the refrigerator or a door. Nope. He went for the gusto.

The frog, with great zeal, was pitched up at the ceiling. That would be, of course, the freshly painted, bright, clean, white ceiling. And there he stuck. About an hour later, Mom was notified, at which point Froggy made a rapid descent at the blunt end of a broomstick. But lest he be forgotten, Sir Froggy left his unmistakably amphibian imprint right in the middle of the gorgeous new kitchen.

Now. Here is where we get to the last, and most necessary, "good thing" any Asperkid's home needs. The single most important tool at your disposal when setting up your home is… (drumroll, please) perspective. **To best serve your Asperkid, yes, you must strive to create a home that is thoughtful, organized, calm, and lovely.**

AND…

It also has to be the place where you can roll with the punches. Where you can show, by example, that sometimes even the best-laid plans get a little sticky. And where, when your Asperkid DOES have a meltdown on the same day you've failed to stock the kids' snack pantry, you do NOT consider yourself the failure who is to blame for every tough day to come. That's just not reality.

A year later, there is still a frog print on my ceiling. Yep, I have the leftover paint to cover him up. But I doubt I will.

Froggy is a reminder of the fact that even the most organized, wonderful family has very "human" moments. He's also a reminder (especially on those days that I have to push myself to calmly say, "Have you checked your routine?" for the hundredth time) that childhood is fleeting. Someday, there won't be three Asperkids running around here in Mommy's too-big high heels or plastic superhero masks.

A calm, orderly house will, undoubtedly, be a lot easier to manage then—it can be tough these days. But I'm fairly certain this home will never be any happier than it is now, with three young (high-maintenance but much-beloved) tornadoes in the kitchen… and a frog print on the ceiling.

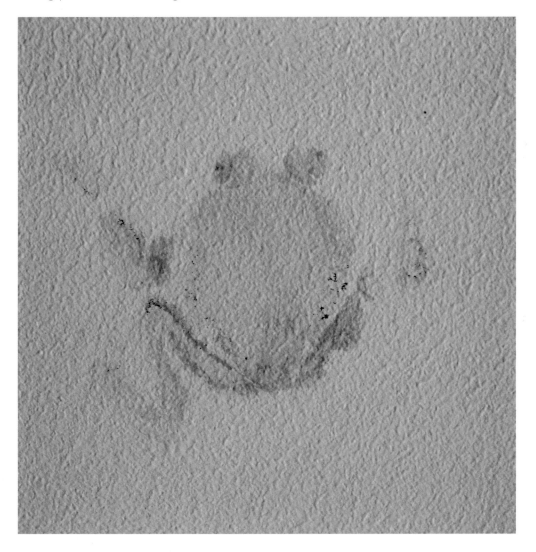

SOME BASIC KITCHEN SAFETY REMINDERS (BECAUSE A LITTLE REMINDER NEVER HURT ANYONE)

1. Check that the oven and other cooking appliances are turned off before you leave the kitchen.

2. Keep electrical appliances away from water to avoid shocks. Stay away from electrical sockets, especially if your hands are wet.

3. If you do burn yourself, hold the burned area under cool running water. Be sure you know where the first aid kit is located.

4. Don't put knives or other sharp objects into a sink full of water. Someone could reach in and get hurt.

5. Be sure you've been taught how to use any tool, appliance, or utensil before you try it on your own.

6. Never put water on a cooking fire—it could make the fire bigger. Put out a fire with a fire extinguisher. If the fire is small, it can be put out with baking soda or smothered with a lid. If the fire has leaping flames, shout to anyone else in the

house to get out—then together, leave the house for a neighbor's home. Call the emergency services immediately.

7. Don't put cooked food on an unwashed plate or cutting board that held raw food. Always use a clean plate.

8. Never add water to a pan that has hot oil in it. It could make the oil splatter.

9. Always turn pot handles in toward the back of the range. This way no one can bump into them and knock the pot over.

10. Keep paper towels, dish towels, and pot holders away from the range so they don't catch fire.

ASPERKID DESIGN RESOURCES

ASPERKID ONLINE INSPIRATION

"The Asperkids Collection" by Montessori Services
www.Asperkids.com/ms

I am so PROUD to present the Asperkids Collection by Montessori Services, a road to confidence and independence for kids with Asperger Syndrome, autism—and every other "typical" child, too. With you in mind, every single item in this collection has been "chosen, celebrated, and personally used" because I trust them and have seen what a difference quality, appropriately sized basics make. Manageable push brooms, woven baskets, lock boxes, expertly grouped activity sets, and even the mini-juice pitcher my kids adore, every item is beautiful and important. Best of all, though, **a portion of all Collection sales will directly fund the work we do on behalf of Asperkids everywhere.**

Pinterest, Asperkids Boards: "Launch Pad" and "Taking Asperkids into the Great Wide Open"
http://pinterest.com/Asperkids/the-asperkid-s-launch-pad
http://pinterest.com/Asperkids/taking-asperkids-into-the-great-wide-open

Constantly updated, these are snapshots of my favorite ideas and inspirations for preparing your superhero's heart and home. Every "pin" (picture) will link you back to its original blog, magazine, or video source.

MORE GOOD STUFF ONLINE

FlipFold
www.flipfold.com

I discovered this gizmo while watching Asperger poster-child Sheldon Cooper fold his laundry on TV's *The Big Bang Theory*, and have never looked back. You only have to see it to understand why the FlipFold (and its jewelry and cosmetic organizer cousins) is a precision-loving, all-thumbs-having, clutter-prone Asperkid's dream.

IHeart Organizing
http://iheartorganizing.blogspot.com

This blog is written by a mom who declares: "Whenever I go missing, it's probably a safe bet that I could be found digging in a cabinet, drawer or closet, paring things down, rearranging and spinning my gears. Always looking at each and every space, wondering what could be done to beautify and simplify that zone." Full of printables, neat ideas, and usable tips, it is definitely a site to bookmark.

Kids' Gardening Online (by the National Gardening Association)
www.kidsgardening.org

Promoting home, school, and community gardening as a means to renew and sustain the essential connections between people, plants, and the environment.

Martha Stewart Online
www.marthastewart.com

I'm not saying that you have to (or even that you should try to) make some homemade soap before your Asperkid's next occupational therapy appointment. But Martha DOES know a good thing when she sees it. That's why it really is worth your while to check out her homekeeping and organizing boards for clever tricks, printables, and checklists.

Office Playground (USA)
www.officeplayground.com

and

I Want One of Those (UK)
www.iwantoneofthose.com

Completely crazy collections of stress balls, tabletop Zen gardens, liquid motion toys, fidgets, and kinetic motion toys to de-stress any Asperkid (and quite possibly Mom and Dad, too).

Real Simple Magazine Online
www.realsimple.com/home-organizing/index.html

"The best tips for cleaning and organizing your home including garages, closets, kitchens, bathrooms." (And yes, they really are good!)

Time Timers
www.timetimer.com

We love the Time Timer! Available as tablet or smartphone apps or as the old standard—actual desktop clocks—the Time Timer is the ultimate tool for visual thinkers, like Aspies (they even won the coveted Asperkid Seal of Awesomeness). When attention issues and less-than-strong organizational skills make it hard for your Asperkid to understand impending transitions (like leaving for school or finishing up screen time), this is a no-brainer. Countdowns are more understandable, and kids feel more prepared. Goodbye frantic freak-outs—hello, Time Timer!

BOOKS

All of these books are available through the Asperkids Collection at www.Asperkids.com/ms (I own them ALL—so I can promise that they are fantastic).

101 Places You Gotta See Before You're 12!
by Joanne O'Sullivan

This must-have book is a field trip, a family vacation, and an eye-opening exercise in appreciating your own backyard all rolled into one. This "untravel" guide suggests visiting a local landfill, the house where your parents grew up, an antiquarian book store…

At Home with Montessori
by Patricia Oriti, illustrated by Julia Sheehan-Burke

A simple picture book about re-imagining the home as a collective success for adults and multi-age children.

Nature's Playground: Activities, Crafts and Games to Encourage Children to Get Outdoors
by Fiona Danks

Lofty ideas and down-to-earth activities and projects for all ages: make paints from natural pigments, freeze up an ice mobile, find six ways to play with mud, explore herb and flower scents.

Tidy Up! (a Small World book)
by Gwenyth Swain

Whether children live in Indonesia or Indiana, "Messes look like mountains until someone lends a hand." This fascinating glimpse of children around the globe going about their daily tasks illustrates the value of caring for ourselves and our immediate environment. As they see how others around the world accomplish the very same tasks, your children will be encouraged to work on their new skills.

GAMES

Both of these companies are winners of the Asperkids Seal of Awesomeness—so you *know* we love them!

Mindware Toys
www.mindware.com

"Brainy Toys for Kids of All Ages."

ThinkFun Games
www.thinkfun.com

"Ignite Your Mind!"